The Canadian
Babysitter's
HANDBOOK

IN ASSOCIATION WITH   St. John Ambulance Saint-Jean

The Canadian
Babysitter's
HANDBOOK

Caroline Greene

RANDOM HOUSE OF CANADA

DK

A DORLING KINDERSLEY BOOK

Editor
Lisa Minsky

Designer
Glenda Tyrrell

Managing Editor
Jemima Dunne

Managing Art Editor
Philip Gilderdale

Canadian Editors
St. John Ambulance, Kathryn Mulders

Deputy Art Director
Tina Vaughan

DTP Designer
Karen Ruane

Production
Maryann Rogers

Photography
Steve Gorton

First Canadian Edition, 1995
2 4 6 8 10 9 7 5 3 1
Published in Canada by
Random House of Canada Limited, Toronto.

Greene, Caroline, 1958–
    The Canadian babysitter's handbook

Includes index.
ISBN 0-394-22481-7

1. Babysitting – Handbooks, manuals, etc. 2. First aid in
illness and injury – Handbooks, manuals, etc. 3. Children's
accidents – Prevention – Handbooks, manuals, etc. I. St. John
Ambulance. II. Title.

HQ769.5.G74 1995   649'.1'0248   C95–931141-6

Manufactured in China by Imago.

Publisher's note
Throughout this book, the pronouns "he" and
"she" refer to both sexes, except where
a topic applies specifically to a boy or girl.

The term "parents" refers to parents,
a parent, or a guardian.

CONTENTS

BABY AND CHILD CARE 15–44

HOME SAFETY
AND FIRST AID 45–78

RECORD AND
LOGBOOK 81–88

INTRODUCTION

St. John Ambulance is dedicated to the mission of helping Canadians improve their health, safety, and quality of life by providing training and community service. We are therefore pleased to cooperate with Random House of Canada on the publication of *The Canadian Babysitter's Handbook*.

This handbook provides necessary information for babysitters – from proper baby and child care techniques, and essential emergency and first aid information, to suggestions for games and toys for various groups. The book is colorful, easy-to-read, and it will be a valuable asset to parents and young people.

While *The Canadian Babysitter's Handbook* is a useful guide and tool, there is no substitute for proper and complete training. St. John Ambulance has provided babysitting training to thousands, and we highly recommend young people take a babysitting as well as a first aid course before accepting their first position as a babysitter. Contact your local St. John Ambulance office to find out more about the courses we offer.

With guidance and training, babysitting can be fun, safe and rewarding for both parents and babysitters. St. John Ambulance hopes that this book will help signpost the way to stress-free babysitting and provide peace of mind for everyone involved.

Eric L. Barry
Chancellor
THE ORDER OF ST. JOHN

GUIDE
TO
BABYSITTING

This first section provides guidelines for both parents and babysitters. For parents, there is advice on choosing a babysitter, information on the parents' responsibilities, a checklist to look at with the babysitter, and tips on evaluating the babysitter. For the babysitter, there is guidance on choosing families, negotiating with parents, meeting children, and assessing the arrangement.

FINDING A BABYSITTER

LOOKING FOR A babysitter can be stressful. Many parents rely on friends or relatives, but there may be times when you need a new babysitter. Invite someone who has been recommended to you home to meet the children before making a commitment. If you and the children like the babysitter, and you think she or he is responsible enough to cope with everyday and unexpected events, ask them to come for a trial run. It is your responsibility as the parent to satisfy yourself that the babysitter will act responsibly and safeguard the well-being of your children and the security of your home. Although age is by no means the only factor you should consider, the St. John Ambulance advises all parents to choose someone who is at least twelve years old.

Children have a say
It is important that your children are also happy with the babysitting arrangement.

YOUR RESPONSIBILITIES

You should agree on the rate and hours with the babysitter before she babysits. Discuss how you would like her to treat your home, show her around, and tell her about the children's routines. Leave a number where she can contact you, the numbers of two relatives or friends, and the address of a neighbor. Prepare young children for bed before she arrives and be realistic about the time you intend to get home. Call her if you are going to be late, and pay her in full, plus extra if you have been longer than agreed. Take her home or pay for a taxi.

If a child is ill, cancel the babysitter. If he is taking a prescribed course of treatment that, given the nature of the treatment and the needs of your child, can be administered by the babysitter, leave a dated note authorizing the babysitter to give the medication, and clear written instructions on how to do it.

WHAT TO EXPECT OF YOUR BABYSITTER

When you leave your children with a babysitter, you can expect him to act responsibly. He should only babysit if he is well and should arrive in good time so that the children are settled before you leave. You can ask him to put them to bed and check on them regularly. He should not smoke or drink, and should use the telephone only in an emergency. If he feels unwell during the job, he should contact you, and you should come home immediately. Don't expect him to carry out household tasks such as cleaning, but he should clean up after himself.

WHAT TO TELL YOUR BABYSITTER

IN AN EMERGENCY	▦ The telephone number you can be contacted at. ▦ Telephone numbers or addresses of two relatives or friends who will be at home while you are out, and the address of a neighbor. ▦ The best route to take out of the home in an emergency.	▦ The telephone numbers of the doctor, the police station, and the local hospital. ▦ Clear written directions on how to get to your home, in case they are needed for the emergency services. ▦ Where to find a fire blanket or a fire extinguisher.
HOME SAFETY	▦ Where the family's first aid kit is kept. ▦ Whether there is a baby monitor and how to use it.	▦ Where the circuit breaker and water shutoff are, and how to operate them. ▦ Where to find a flashlight.
TOYS AND ACTIVITIES	▦ The toys you would like your children to play with. ▦ The games that you would like the children to play, and those to avoid before bedtime.	▦ The television programs or videos that your children are allowed to watch. ▦ Whether older children are allowed to use the telephone.
BEDTIME	▦ The bedtime routine for each child and where to tell them bedtime stories. ▦ What time lights are turned out and if there is a nightlight. ▦ Whether bedroom doors are left open or closed.	▦ What to do if children wake up during the evening. ▦ Where extra blankets and clothing are kept. ▦ If the children sleepwalk, sleeptalk, or suffer from nightmares, and what to do.
HEALTH AND BEHAVIOR	▦ Whether the children have been ill recently. ▦ If they are allergic to food, medication, adhesive bandages, or have any medical condition.	▦ Any characteristic behavior that might need to be explained. ▦ What to do if children misbehave and how to deal with misbehavior.
FOOD	▦ Where feeding equipment is kept and what the children can eat and drink.	▦ How to burp the baby after a bottle.

BECOMING A BABYSITTER

I F YOU DECIDE that you would like to babysit, ask friends or relatives to recommend you to families. You could also contact your local primary school where teachers may know of families who need babysitters. It is best to depend on word-of-mouth since you and the family will feel more confident if you have been recommended to each other. Choose a family with whom you feel comfortable and make sure that you are happy with the babysitting arrangements.

WHAT TO DISCUSS WITH PARENTS

Before you agree to babysit for a new family, arrange to meet the parents and children at their home to discuss the details of the babysitting arrangements. This will prevent any embarrassment or confusion later on, and you will feel more confident about what is expected of you. It is also a good opportunity for you and the children to get to know each other. Ask the parents for a brief outline of the children's routines, likes, and dislikes, and find out whether the children have any allergies or medical conditions, such as asthma.

NEGOTIATING RATES

Find out the local rate before going to meet the family. Tell them that you are charging the going rate and make it clear whether you are charging by the hour or by the evening, and whether you charge extra if the babysitting continues after midnight.

If you know the family and have been asked to stay for the night, negotiate an overnight charge. You may also decide to charge a higher rate if you are looking after more than a certain number of children.

Some parents may want to negotiate a rate, so decide for yourself the minimum rate that you would accept. It is also a good idea to agree on a rate for extra time in case the parents get back late. Keep your rates consistent so that other families know what to expect if you are recommended to them. Make it clear that you expect to be paid in full at the end of each session, including any time over the agreed length.

Agreeing to babysit

Once you have agreed to babysit for a new family, clarify the hours you will be spending there and the amount you will be paid. If you don't want to babysit late during the week, make this clear to the parents when you meet them.

You should also ask the parents to spend some time showing you where everything is kept, such as any diaper changing equipment, the telephone, if there is one, the first aid kit, if they have one, and the thermometer.

Ask the parents to leave a number where you can contact them if possible, numbers to call in an emergency, the numbers of two friends or relatives, and the address of a neighbor who will be in while you are babysitting. This address is especially important if the home where you are babysitting does not have a telephone.

WHAT YOU NEED TO ASK

Before you babysit for a family

▦ The number of children. Do they all belong to the same family?

▦ The names and ages of the children.

▦ What you should do if a child should misbehave.

▦ The amount you will be paid, and whether it is by the hour or for the whole evening.

▦ Whether you might be expected to help the children with homework.

▦ What time the children go to bed and their bedtime routines.

▦ If any of the children have a medical condition such as diabetes, epilepsy, or asthma, and the routine to follow if they do have an attack.

▦ If there are any pets and whether they need to be fed.

Each time you babysit

▦ The starting and finishing time of the babysitting job.

▦ Whether there are any changes in the routine from the last time.

▦ Whether you are expected to feed the children, and where they eat.

Further questions
Prepare a list of questions before you go to the parents and review the list together.

▦ Which activities the parents want you to do with the children, and where.

▦ Whether the children will be in bed when you arrive, or whether you will be expected to put them to bed.

▦ Where the parents can be contacted.

▦ The numbers and addresses of two friends or relatives and a neighbor for you to contact in an emergency.

What about you?

▦ How you will get there and how you will get home.

▦ Can you make yourself something to eat or drink?

▦ Can you use the television or VCR, or do homework?

▦ Can you bring a friend? Wait until you have done several babysitting jobs for a family before you ask.

MEETING THE CHILDREN

It is sensible to meet the children with their parents before you babysit. This will give you the opportunity to make friends with the children in their home environment and also means that they will already know you when you do come to babysit.

Before you babysit

Although you will be eager to establish a good relationship with the children, if you push yourself upon them, you will risk frightening or intimidating them. Instead, take along a few things that you think might interest them in a "magic bag," (see page 38). Sit on the floor with the children and play with some of the items that you have brought with you. The children will soon overcome their shyness and will want to see what you are doing. If they don't show any interest at first, try to join in gradually with their activities. You could also ask them to show you their room or tell you which toys are their favorites. Ask them which games they like playing and what else they like to do.

Keeping the children happy

When you meet the children again, they may act differently. Knowing that their parents are going out, they may be upset or overexcited, and older children may be unfriendly. They should recover once their parents have gone. As the parents leave, try to engage children in a story, activity or video, or bring out your "magic bag" – that way, they will feel that they are doing something special too. If a child is really unhappy, comfort him and contact his parents if possible.

Babysitting regularly

If the children are happy with you, it is likely that the parents will ask you to babysit again. Once you become a regular babysitter, you will build up a relationship with the children and become part of their lives.

Joining in
Sit on the floor with the children and join in with their game, or bring along other items that they might enjoy playing with.

YOUR RESPONSIBILITIES

arents are responsible for providing a
afe and secure environment for you to
abysit in. However, you may be also
eld liable if you endanger a child's
ealth or safety. For your own safety,
ell *your* parents who you are babysitting
or and give them the family's address
nd, if they have one, the family's
elephone number. Tell your parents
hat time you expect to be home and
elephone them if this changes.

you feel ill

Don't babysit if you are ill – you won't
e able to do your job properly and you
nay infect the children. Give the parents
s much notice as possible so that they
ave some time to find a replacement
abysitter. If you start feeling ill while
ou are babysitting, contact the
arents and ask them to come home.

efore the parents leave

rrive at least 15 minutes before the
arents want to leave so that you have
me to talk about any relevant concerns.
Check that they have left you their
elephone number or a way to contact
hem, and other contact numbers or
ddresses in case there is an emergency.

Doubtful situations

Never leave the children alone in the
ouse, even for 30 seconds. If a crisis
r worrying situation arises – perhaps
here have been strange telephone calls
r the baby won't stop crying – don't
eel you have to cope on your own.
f you're unsure or unhappy about
nything, telephone the parents, your
arents, or one of the contact numbers.
Never risk your own safety or that
f the children in your care.

Comforting a child
*If a child does not seem
happy, comfort and
reassure her, and find
something to do that will
distract her.*

Taking your responsibilities seriously

If you are doing homework or watching
a video while babysitting, this must take
second place to your responsibilities
as a babysitter. Keep the volume low
if you have the television or music on
so that you can hear if the children wake
up. Check babies and children regularly,
and comfort a child if he is upset. You
should stay awake throughout.

Don't smoke or drink alcohol, and use
the telephone only in a crisis. Also, be
aware of safety in the home (see pages
45 to 50), and let the parents know if
any incidents have occurred.

Respect your agreements with the
parents and don't invite friends over
without their permission. Clean up
after yourself and leave the home as
it was when you arrived.

EVALUATING THE BABYSITTING ARRANGEMENT

I T IS IN THE interests of the parents, children, and the babysitter to make a success of the babysitting arrangement. If everyone feels comfortable with it, then it is worth continuing. As the family and the babysitter get to know one another the arrangement becomes easier.

ASSESSING YOUR BABYSITTER

Although you are not going to be able to watch the babysitter in your home, the following points will enable you to evaluate the success of the babysitting arrangement.

Other opinions
Your children will want to tell you what they think of the babysitter.

• What did the babysitter report back to you and what did your children tell you about the babysitter?
• Were you told about any incidents? If so, could they have been prevented?
• Are the children tired, suggesting that they went to bed late?
• If you tell your children that the same babysitter is coming back, how do they react?
• If you use the same person a few times, are the children pleased or do they become nervous and uneasy?
• Is the babysitter happy with the babysitting arrangements?

WAS YOUR BABYSITTING SUCCESSFUL?

Think of your first time babysitting as a trial run and remember that it gets easier as you become familiar with the home and children. If you feel uncomfortable with the arrangements in any way, try to discuss this with the parents, and talk to your own parents or friends if you are concerned. If you are still unsure, trust your instincts and turn the parents down if they ask you to babysit again. Consider the following points before you agree to another job.

• Were you made aware of domestic arrangements and the children's needs?
• Were you left contact numbers?
• Did you get along with the children?
• Did the parents return when they said they would?
• How did they react when you told them about misbehavior or incidents?
• Were you satisfied with the arrangements made for paying you?
• Were you happy with the arrangements for getting home?

BABY
AND
CHILD CARE

Children will often be ready for bed or in bed before you arrive, but there may be times when parents ask you to help a child wash or to change a diaper. This section includes everything you need to know about basic baby and child care from picking up a baby to helping a toddler use a potty. It also has ideas for entertaining children.

HOLDING AND HANDLING

BE GENTLE AND confident when you handle a young baby. If he feels secure, he is less likely to be upset at being away from his parents.

Support a baby's whole body when you hold him. Be careful not to let his head flop and not to put pressure on the top of his scalp.

PICKING UP A BABY

Support the baby's head at all times

3 Transfer his head to the crook of your elbow, or to your shoulder, so that his head and limbs feel fully supported.

2 Gently lift him from the surface, making sure that his head doesn't fall back. Reassure him by talking to him quietly as you lift him.

1 Slide one hand under his lower back and the other under his neck and head.

PUTTING DOWN A BABY

1 Hold him with one hand under his head and neck and the other hand under his bottom. Lower him gently.

Cradle his head and neck with one hand

2 When his weight is fully supported by the flat surface, gently slide your hand out from under his bottom.

3 Then use your free hand to raise his head just enough for you to release your other hand. Lower his head back down gently.

PLAYING WITH AND CARRYING A BABY

Once babies are strong enough to hold up their own heads (at about three months) they can be entertained as they are held. A baby will enjoy being carried in different ways, and you will be able to play games with him as you hold him.

PLAYING

Support his body with both hands

Sitting on your lap
This is a favorite position for playing singing and bouncing games. Face him toward you and hold him firmly around his waist or under his arms.

Always talk to the baby

Holding a baby upright
He may enjoy being held upright, with his face at eye level, while you support him.

CARRYING

Sitting on your hip
He can show an interest in what's happening around him if you use both hands to support him astride your hip. Put one hand under his bottom and the other around his waist.

Rocking
Lie the baby along your forearm, supporting his back with your other hand, and rock him gently to and fro. Singing as you do this can soothe a crying baby.

Forward-facing carry
You can use both hands to hold the baby with his back against your body so that he has a good view as well as reassuring body contact.

Put one hand across his chest and the other under his bottom

17

UNDRESSING AND DRESSING

BABY

Have everything nearby before you dress or undress the baby and never leave her once you have started. Make sure that she feels secure and is lying on a flat surface such as a changing table or bed. Be confident but gentle. Keep her happy by constantly smiling and talking, and don't let her get cold.

UNDRESSING

1 Undo the snaps of the stretchie. Guide one ankle out of the stretchie leg. Repeat with the other.

Hold her gently and do not jerk her

Pull the outfit, not her foot

2 Hold her elbow inside the sleeve. Pull off the sleeve by the cuff. Repeat with the other arm. Lift the baby and pull away the outfit, or ease it from under her.

3 Pull the undershirt up over her tummy. Hold her elbow inside the fabric and ease the undershirt ove[r] her fist. Repeat with her other arm.

4 Gather up the undershi[rt] in both your hands and stretch it wide. Quickly lift it over her face.

DRESSING

1 Gather the undershirt and open the neck wide. Gently pull it over the baby's head.

2 Make sure you protect the baby's fingers with your hand as you guide one of her arms through a sleeve. Pull the undershirt down, then repeat with the other arm.

Undo all the snaps before you start

Pull the leg onto the baby's leg

3 Lay the baby on the open stretchie. Ease the stretchie legs on first, one at a time.

4 Guide the arm through, as with the undershi[rt] Do up the snaps working from the bottom upward.

TODDLER

Toddlers often like to show their growing independence by choosing their clothes and putting them on. Be patient, and let her do as much as she can by herself to keep undressing and dressing from becoming a battle.

UNDRESSING

Toddlers find it easier to undress than to dress, but you will need to be patient. First help her undo all the fastenings, then let her pull everything off. You can make a game of it, although if she is getting ready for bed, don't get her too excited as it will almost certainly be more difficult to settle her down. She may enjoy being without clothes and want to run around with nothing on, but encourage her to put on her pajamas as the next part of the game.

Getting undressed
Buttons can be particularly challenging for small fingers.

DRESSING

As a babysitter, you will generally be getting children ready for bed, but there may be situations where you will need to help them get dressed or changed.

Allow yourself plenty of time, so that you won't feel rushed, and lay out her clothes in order before you start. It might be easier to sit a small toddler on your knee and help her.

Make a story out of what she is doing. You can talk about her hands going on a journey through the sleeves and out the other side, or her feet making a nest in her shoes. Alternatively, make a game out of dressing by playing "peek-a-boo," or counting to see how many numbers she takes to put on each item. For difficult fastenings, such as laces, ask her to start them, then finish them for her.

Dressing for bed
Encourage a reluctant child to dress by making it a game.

DIAPERS, POTTIES, AND TOILETS

CHANGING A DIAPER

Before putting the baby on the changing pad, wash your hands. *Never* leave the baby alone on a table. Talk or sing to her, and let her kick and play before you put on the new diaper.

WHAT DO I NEED?

- Clean diaper
- Cotton balls or baby wipes
- Warm water
- Baby powder
- Baby ointment

CLEANING A BOY

1 Undo the dirty diaper and hold it over his penis in case he wets himself. Open out the diaper and wipe away any mess. Fold the front of the diaper under his bottom.

Wipe toward his bottom as you clean his penis

2 Moisten a cotton ball in warm water, or use wipes, and clean his tummy. Use fresh cotton balls or wipes to clean his penis and leg creases.

3 Lift his legs to clean his bottom. Discard the dirty diaper. Dry him with wipes and powder him. Apply ointment ov his lower tummy and th whole diaper area.

CLEANING A GIRL

1 Open the diaper and wipe away any mess. Fold the diaper down under her bottom.

2 Moisten some cotton balls with warm water, or use wipes, and wipe her tummy. Use fresh cotton or wipes to clean her leg creases, wiping downward, away from her body.

Clean up to her belly button

Avoid wiping the inside of her vaginal lips, unless she is soiled

3 Lift her legs and wipe her bottom from front to back. Remove the diaper and dry her with wipes. Pu ointment on the diaper are:

PUTTING ON A DISPOSABLE DIAPER

Many parents use disposable diapers for their babies. When you find out where all the diaper-changing equipment is kept, ask where you should dispose of the dirty diapers. Never put disposable diapers down the toilet.

1 After cleaning the baby (see opposite), wipe your hands, making sure you clean off any ointment. Gently lift the baby by her ankles and slide the open diaper under her until the top edge aligns with her waist.

Make sure the tapes are at the top

Keep one finger between her ankles to keep them from rubbing

2 Pull the front up and spread it over her tummy. Hold one corner in position.

3 With the other hand, unpeel the tape and stick it over the diaper front. Repeat for the other corner.

4 Check that the diaper is not twisted and is snug – there should just be room for one finger between the diaper and the baby's waist. If necessary, open the tapes and reposition them to adjust the fit. If a diaper tape does not stick, try adhesive tape, if there is any, or replace the diaper.

Turn the top of the waistband down if it rubs her tummy

DIAPERS, POTTIES, AND TOILETS

PUTTING ON A CLOTH DIAPER

If parents use cloth diapers, they should have a few ready for use, along with a convenient supply of pins or diaper wraps. Make sure that the parents show you where you should put the dirty diapers after changing the baby.

Make sure the top is level with the waist

1 Clean the baby's bottom thoroughly and put on the ointment (see page 20). Lift the baby's legs and slide the diaper under her bottom, lining up the top edge with her waist. If there are diaper liners, place one under the baby's bottom in the center of the diaper.

Lift her gently by the ankles

Hold the two pieces together

3 Pull over the other corner. Hold it together with one hand and fasten the diaper pin with the other. Keep your fingers behind the pin, so it does not pass through the fabric and poke the baby.

2 Bring the center of the diaper up between her legs. Hold the diaper in position and bring one side of it over to the center, pulling it slightly to keep the diaper fitting closely.

OLDER BABY

You will have to adapt the above technique for an older or larger baby. Bring the center of the diaper up as before, then lift one corner and pin it in place. Repeat on the other side.

For a larger baby, put a pin in each corner

POTTY OR TOILET TRAINING

f you are babysitting a toddler, it is likely that he is at some stage of potty training. Ask his parents what he will say when he needs to go to the potty or the bathroom, and find out how the parents ask him if he needs to go. You may have to wait with him for a time before he does anything. It may help to take a toy or a book with you. Pretend teddy also has to go to the bathroom, or amuse the child with a story. Praise the toddler each time he uses the potty.

Sitting on the potty
Make sure she sits on the potty the right way around.

Unhurried potty time
Be patient when he is using the potty and don't rush him.

A toddler or older child who prefers to use the toilet will be independent about doing so, but check whether he would like any help. You may need to unzip his pants, wipe his bottom, or help to flush. If he uses a step and child's toilet seat, check that these are in place. Remind the child to wash his hands afterward. Before bed, remind him to use the potty or toilet as usual.

MISHAPS

Never get angry with a child if he has a mishap. It may have happened because he is feeling insecure without his parents. If he is wearing training pants you will be saved from a mess, but if a mishap occurs, lay him down to clean him or stand him in the bath on a non-slip mat to wash his bottom.

Toilet safety
She may need help fitting the safety seat over the toilet or climbing onto it. Check that the seat is secure before she uses it.

WASHING

WASHING A BABY'S FACE AND BOTTOM

You may be asked to wash the baby. This means washing her hands, face, neck, and diaper area. Wash your hands, ensure the room is warm, and strip her down to her underwear (see page 18).

WHAT DO I NEED?

- Two bowls of lukewarm water
- Hooded baby towel
- Cotton balls or soft baby washcloth
- Baby ointment

Use a fresh cotton ball for each wipe

1 Wipe each eye from the nose outward with cotton balls dipped in warm water, or a washcloth. Wipe over and behind each ear. Next, wipe around her mouth and nose.

Clean in her neck creases carefully

2 Wipe over her cheeks and forehead and under her chin. Pat her face dry with a towel.

3 Wipe under her arms and dry them thoroughly. Wipe between her fingers and over her hands.

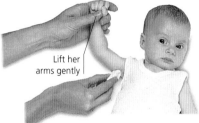

Lift her arms gently

4 Undo the baby's diaper and clean her bottom (see page 20). Apply baby ointment and put on a clean diaper (pages 21 to 22). Always wash the baby beginning with her face and ending with her bottom.

Always wipe from front to back

24

HELPING A YOUNG CHILD WASH

A toddler or young child will probably need some encouragement to wash before bedtime. Help her to reach the sink – she may use a step – and fill the sink with water for her. Make sure that the water is not too hot. If she really doesn't want to wash, try to persuade her to use a damp washcloth for a quick wipe. Make a game out of washing – try not to lose your temper or let washing become a battle.

BRUSHING HAIR

Find out whether hair brushing is part of the bedtime routine. A toddler may want to brush her own hair, although you might have to help her brush in the right direction and help her get all the tangles out. Brush the hair gently – some children have very sensitive scalps. Parents should not expect you to wash their child's hair when you are babysitting.

She may want to show you how she brushes her hair

Brushing teeth
Give her lots of praise
when she brushes
her teeth.

CLEANING TEETH

Remind older children to brush their teeth before they go to bed. Toddlers and young children will need your help. You may have to sit a toddler on your lap and gently brush her teeth for her. Alternatively, you could ask her to show you how good she is at cleaning her teeth or play a game of you both watching her in the mirror. After she has cleaned her teeth, get her to rinse her mouth and spit out any toothpaste.

FEEDING

PREPARING A BABY'S BOTTLE

The parents should make up the bottles you will need for the baby, but if they want you to do it, ask how to prepare a bottle and where the equipment is. Wash your hands before making up a bottle.

WHAT DO I NEED?

▪ Sterilized bottles, rings, nipples, & disks
▪ Boiled water
▪ Formula powder/ ready-to-use formula and butter knife

USING BABY FORMULA POWDER

Check the measure at eye level

2 Use the scoop provided with the formula to scoop up the powder. Drop the powder into the water and repeat for the recommended number of scoops.

3 Tightly screw on the disk and ring. Shake the bottle well. Remove the ring and take out the disk. Put the nipple in the ring, slipping it in from beneath. Allow the formula to cool.

1 Pour fresh, cooled boiled water into the sterilized bottle, to the right measure. Avoid touching the nipple.

Level off the scoop with a butter knife

USING READY-TO-USE FORMULA

If the mother has left bottled breast milk for the baby, start with step 2.

Scrub the top of the container

1 Make sure the top of the container is clean. Cut off the top corner and pour the milk into a sterilized bottle.

The bottle will take about a minute to warm up

2 Stand the bottle in a bowl of very hot water to heat it until it is lukewarm (see opposite).

GIVING A BOTTLE

efore giving the baby a bottle, wash your hands. heck that the bottle is at the right temperature. tand a prepared bottle in a bowl of boiled water heat it. Don't use a microwave – it's dangerous ecause it will heat the formula unevenly. Test milk by shaking a few drops onto the ont of your wrist. It should feel lukewarm.

2 When he begins to suck, hold the bottle firmly and tilt it so the nipple is full of milk and free of air. If the nipple gets stuck together, move the bottle around his mouth. He will keep sucking until he has had enough. An older baby may want to hold his own bottle.

Put a bib on the baby to protect his clothes

Hold the baby with his back supported along our forearm and his head sting in the crook of your bow. Keep his head raised ightly so that he can suck nd swallow easily.

Tilt the bottle to keep the nipple full

URPING A BABY

If a baby dozes off or pauses while feeding, he may have swallowed air and will need "burping": put a cloth over your shoulder and hold him against it (see left), or sit him upright. He will soon burp if he has swallowed air. Offer him the bottle again after he burps in case he is still hungry. If he wants more, don't forget to burp him again when he is finished.

Against your shoulder
Put him against your shoulder and gently rub or pat his back.

Sitting on your lap
Lean him forward slightly, support his chin, and gently rub or pat his back.

FEEDING

FEEDING A YOUNG BABY

FROM 4 – 6 MONTHS

From about four months old, babies may start to try "solids" – these are often small amounts of baby cereal or puréed fruit or vegetables. The parents will tell you if they would like you to give the baby solids, what you should give her, and how much. They may ask you to give her a bottle at the same time.

Before feeding a baby, put a bib on her to protect her clothes. Give her a little food on the tip of a plastic spoon and let her suck it. Don't worry if she only eats a little; she is still having bottles. Keep paper towels nearby to mop up spills.

Feeding from a spoon
Sit the baby on your lap or in a baby chair. Offer her the tip of the spoon.

FROM 5 – 6 MONTHS

At this age a baby may have started to eat "finger foods," such as pieces of banana. The parents will tell you if they want you to give him anything to eat and what you should give him. *Never* experiment with new foods or give him dry foods such as chips – they could make him gag or choke. The parents may ask you to give him a drink from a training cup – if so, you will probably need to hold it

Eating finger foods
Make sure you stay with him all the time while he is eating, even if he doesn't seem to need help.

FEEDING AN OLDER BABY

ROM 7 – 15 MONTHS

y seven months old, a baby is actively
king part in feeding. It can be a messy
ocess, so if the parents ask you to feed
r, use a large bib and have
per towels nearby.

Keep her bowl out of reach at first.
After you have fed her some spoonfuls,
let her experiment with the bowl, but
continue feeding her yourself. Offer
to hold the cup when she drinks.

aying with food
e will enjoy playing
th her food while
u feed her, so
ep paper towels
arby to wipe her
nds and face.

FEEDING TIPS

▥ Never leave a baby or
young child alone while
she is eating.

▥ She is getting used to
textures; her food should be
finely chopped, not puréed.

▥ She may grab at the
spoon while you feed her.
Let her take it, but have
a clean one ready.

▥ Don't put sugar or salt
in food for babies.

Using a cup
Hold and tip her cup
for her – she may not
be able to hold it
properly yet.

ROM 15 MONTHS

om this age, a child can feed himself
sing a spoon or child's fork. The parents
ould tell you what they want him to
eat, although you
will need to chop
his food into
small pieces.

He likes using
his own spoon

eeding himself
e will want to feed himself, but
ep an eye on him while he eats.

YOUNG CHILDREN

By the age of two, a child will often be
out of a high chair, sitting in a raised
seat at the table, and joining in with
ordinary mealtimes. The parents should
tell you if he drinks from a training cup
and if they want you to feed him. If so,
they should have prepared food for him.

Refusal to eat

Don't worry if a toddler refuses to eat
much or any of his meal - it is all part of
his changing pattern; his likes and dislikes
may swing wildly from day to day or
week to week. Don't rush or punish
him since this may discourage him from
eating entirely. If he hasn't eaten at all,
tell his parents when they return. Loss
of appetite may be a sign that a child is ill.

CRYING

FOR BABIES AND young children, crying is a part of their everyday communication. It can be difficult to know why a baby is crying, but it is important to respond quickly. If you leave him, you will only upset him more. You can try sever methods of soothing him.

REASONS FOR CRYING

UP TO 6 MONTHS

When a young baby cries, he is telling you that he needs something. He may be hungry and need feeding, or he might have a dirty diaper that needs to be changed. He may be feeling uncomfortable because he is too hot or too cold. If he is around three months old, he may suffer from colic, and then he will cry until he feels comfortable again. Often he just needs the security of being held and given a cuddle.

Keep calm
Try not to worry if the baby is crying; overreacting may make him cry more.

6 – 12 MONTHS

An older baby will cry when he feels hungry, uncomfortable, or tired, but there may be other reasons why he is crying. As he becomes more aware, he may feel anxious when a parent leaves him. He may also feel frustrated when he starts to try out his new skills. Once an older baby begins crawl, he is more likely to have knocks and bumps that will make him cry eve if they are not serious. Some older babies may also cry when they start teething. Any combination of these things can make a baby tearful and overtired, particularly by the evening.

Crying alone
Don't leave a baby to cry. Try to comfort him, but if he doesn't want to be cuddled, stay nearby and try to distract him with a toy.

YOUNG CHILD

The frustrations a toddler feels as he becomes more independent often give rise to anger and crying. He may also have tantrums (see page 32). Young children may have fears or phobias tha are more likely to upset them if they feel insecure when their parents are ou

HOW TO COMFORT A BABY

If a baby cries even though he has been fed and changed, try soothing him by cuddling him. Hold him upright against your shoulder, or face down along your forearm, and walk around a little (see page 17). Pat his back gently – he will like the rhythm and it may help him to burp – or try wrapping him snugly in a blanket and rocking him in your arms. If he has a pacifier, make sure that it is completely clean and give it to him to suck.

Once the baby starts to calm down, you can distract him by showing him objects such as a mobile or shiny mirror.

Soothe him by talking and singing to him, or put on some quiet music. If the crying becomes loud and uncontrollable and goes on that way for some time, try to contact his parents or another adult. Don't be embarrassed; he may be unwell, and you are acting responsibly by trying to contact them.

Giving comfort
Once he has calmed down, soothe him with your voice or play a quiet game with him.

HOW TO COMFORT A CHILD

When a young child is crying, try to comfort him by attracting his attention. Give him something to look at, such as a storybook, and suggest reading it together, or find a toy or game, and show him how it works.

Feeling better
A young child may have a special teddy bear or security blanket that will comfort her if she feels upset.

If the child is having a tantrum, you will need to let it run its course before he can be distracted (see page 32).

If an older child is crying, suggest doing a jigsaw puzzle or watching a video together, if there is one. Alternatively, ask him to help you do something, such as prepare a cold drink. He will enjoy sharing a little responsibility with you.

BREATH HOLDING

When babies or young children are very upset, they may suddenly hold their breath as they are crying, and may even become stiff and turn blue. Keep calm: a child will usually start breathing again spontaneously.

If a baby holds his breath, blow gently in his face to startle him into breathing. If he loses consciousness, see pages 70 and 74.

CRYING

HOW TO COPE WITH TANTRUMS

Tantrums are most common in toddlers and young children between the ages of 18 months and three years. A tantrum's uncontrollable rage is a result of the child's frustration at not being able to do what she wants to do. The frustration is caused because the child cannot do something herself, or because you have prevented her from doing something for reasons she doesn't understand.

When a child has a tantrum, she cries, screams, kicks, hits, and may even bang her head on the wall or floor. It can last for over 15 minutes and it can be exhausting both for you and the child.

Let the tantrum run its course
It is difficult to reason or tempt a child out of a tantrum since her mind is made up. You need to let the tantrum run its course and make sure that you stay calm throughout.

Clear a space and stay with her
Make sure that she cannot hurt herself or others. Move objects out of her way if she rolls on the floor, for instance. If you are able to hold onto her, do so, since the physical contact may calm her down, but until she has spent her energy you will not be able to distract her.

Do not leave the child alone in this state – talk quietly and reassuringly to her throughout the tantrum.

Calming down
As soon as she quiets down, you can divert or soothe her by taking her hand and leading her into another room to find a toy, a story, or a snack. If you help her to recover now, she will soon forget why she was angry.

After a tantrum
Once she has calmed down, try to distract her. If she doesn't want to play, don't force her, but stay nearby.

ARGUMENTS

hildren frequently argue when a
ounger child tries to join in with the
ctivities of her older brother or sister.
he wants to master what the older
hild is doing, but the older child may
e the interruption as a threat or
mply as a nuisance.
s soon as one child
rotests and the
her argues back,
ey might start
fight.

Tug-of-war
*If children are fighting over
toys or games, distract one
of them with something else,
and explain to them
both about sharing
and taking turns.*

oining in

one of the children wants to play with
e same toy or game as another, try to
in in too, at least until the children
e happily settled together. By joining
with them yourself, you can help
prevent too many arguments by
oosing who does what.

At other times, arguments are likely
flare up when both children want
play with exactly the same thing.
ell the children that they will have to
ke turns and, to begin with, take the
rst turn yourself. That way, neither of
e children will feel that they have lost
t by not being first.

atching television

hen children are arguing about which
levision program or which video they
ant to watch, it is less easy to be a
ffer. You may even have to toss a
in and tell the loser that it will be his
rn to choose next time.

Fighting

With older children, arguments can
quickly flare up into physical fighting.
Ask the parents what you should do
if the children start fighting. Try to be
firm and consistent with the children
– they are more likely to take notice of
you when you try to stop them. The best
way to avoid fights is to divide the
children for a time and to get them
interested in separate activities.

ARGUMENTS WITH YOU

Besides discussing family routines and
expectations with the parents before you
babysit, you should also discuss how you
could prevent or stop an argument.

If an argument between yourself and a
child does occur, make sure you stay calm,
and try to reason with the child. Never hit
a child. If you felt unsure about dealing
with an argument, ask the parents for
advice when they return home.

BEDTIME

PUTTING A YOUNG BABY TO BED

UP TO 6 MONTHS

Whenever you babysit, it is best to keep to the bedtime routines that the parents have told you about. With young babies, however, a routine may be very new and may not work well since babies' sleeping patterns are always changing. Some young babies may be upset by having someone they don't know handling them, so you might find that your success at putting a baby to bed varies.

Sleeping baby
Lay the baby down to sleep on his back or side, and check on him every half hour while he sleeps.

IF THE BABY WAKES

■ If he wakes up and cries, go to him right away. Feed him if it is time for his bottle; otherwise, check whether he needs a new diaper or if he is too hot. When he is comfortable, try to settle him down again.

■ If he is difficult to settle, rock him in your arms or his chair, if he has one, or push him backward and forward in his stroller.

Most young babies sleep after they have been fed. If the baby falls asleep in your arms, take him to his crib and lay him on his side or back, *never* on his front. Check that he is not too hot or cold, or that he is not wearing too many clothes or covered by too many blankets since he may get overheated. Remove any toys or pillows from the crib. Leave the room as it is normally left (see "logbook," page 86).

Settling a baby
Ask the parents if the baby is happy to be put to bed before he falls asleep. If he usually has a pacifier, make sure he has it. If he cries when left, go back and try to soothe him while he is in bed. If he still doesn't relax, pick him up, wrap him securely in a blanket, and cuddle him. Singing to him and rocking him may put him to sleep, so you can put him back in the crib. Once he is asleep, check on him every half hour.

PUTTING AN OLDER BABY TO BED

6 MONTHS – 1 YEAR

Check the baby's nighttime routine with his parents, and see "logbook," page 86. An older baby may have a routine or he may be going through a new phase when he fights the need to go to sleep and doesn't want to go to bed.

Before bedtime

An important part of any older baby's routine is the time before he goes to bed. This needs to be a time when he winds down so that he feels calm and secure when he goes to bed. Ask the parents whether there is a particular storybook that he likes to look at, or a special tape of songs that he listens to. The parents may ask you to give him a bottle of milk before he goes to bed – *never* give him a bottle when he is in his crib.

Baby rituals

Some older babies have particular rituals that the parents will tell you about. You may have to say goodnight to special teddy bears, or to some of the pictures on the wall.

When you put the baby in his crib, make sure he has any comforters that he usually takes with him. This could

Settling down
If he is not ready to go to sleep, settle him in his crib by reading him a story or playing him some relaxing songs.

be a favorite teddy bear or toy, a special blanket, a pacifier, or all of these. If there is a musical crib toy, play a tune for him once he is settled in his crib.

Leaving the room

Before you leave the room, check that the crib sides are fully up and the crib contains no stuffed toys or pillows. The baby may pull himself into a standing position when he wakes up, and any clutter in the crib could act as a step. Ask the parents how you should leave the room; check if you should leave a light on or the door open (see "logbook").

IF THE BABY WAKES

■ If he wakes and cries, go to him right away and soothe him while he is in the crib. He may have had a bad dream, or he could be cold from kicking his cover off.

■ Try tucking him in and giving him his pacifier, if he has one. If he is still unsettled, sing to him or play some relaxing music.

BEDTIME

PUTTING A CHILD TO BED

Before the parents go out, agree on the time for bed – in front of the children. There is less room for argument if a child knows what time he has to go to bed.

Ask the parents about the child's bedtime routine (see "logbook," page 86). Find out if he wears a diaper in bed, when he goes to the bathroom, and if he might wake up, have nightmares, or sleepwalk.

Settle a child into bed
Always take a child to his bedroom and settle him into bed – there is no appeal at all for a child in being sent to his bedroom on his own. If he has been playing happily with you in another part of the house, his bedroom will seem dark and lonely in comparison.

IF A CHILD GETS OUT OF BED

A child may get up again after you have settled him into bed. Take him straight back to bed, reassure him, and read him another story – he may be feeling a little unhappy without his parents there.

If a child refuses to go to bed
It will be difficult to know whether a child's refusal to go to bed is usual, or if it is because the parents are out and he feels insecure. You will need to be firm but sympathetic. Praise him for getting into bed and spend some time with him in his bedroom. Make the bedroom cozy before you leave and wait a few moments outside his bedroom door.

If you really cannot persuade a child to go to bed, let him stay up and play quietly with you, and then try putting him to bed later on. You could suggest making a bed for him on the sofa. If going to bed has been a problem, discuss it with the parents when they return.

Settling in bed
Spend some time settling a child in bed – she may like you to read her a story

Before a child goes to sleep

Keep a child calm and relaxed before he goes to sleep – put on a story tape or songs, or read him a story yourself. Put away any clothes and toys – children will often sleep better if you don't leave the room too quickly.

If a child tries to prolong going to sleep by asking for a drink or something to eat, or by saying that he needs to go to the bathroom again, agree the first time, then be firm about him staying in bed. Tell him that you will come back to say goodnight in ten minutes. Keep your word and go back into the bedroom, but don't repeat this since it will just become a game to him.

Once a child has gone to bed

Make sure that the volume of the stereo or television is turned down low enough for you to hear a child if he is crying or if he calls for you, and don't wear personal headphones.

If a child does get out of bed and comes back to the living room while you are watching television, turn the television off. Not only is it another reason for the child to want to stay up with you, but there may be programs on the television that are upsetting or disturbing for children.

Waking up
Comfort and reassure a child who has woken up during the evening.

IF A CHILD WAKES

A child may be a little confused if he wakes up during the evening. He may ask for his parents and become upset when he realizes they are not there. Give him a hug, but be firm about settling him back down. Sit with him until he feels more comfortable and read him a story if he needs to be distracted. Let the parents know that he woke up when they return home.

Nightmares

If a child has a nightmare, he may be too scared to sleep. Take time to reassure him. Tell his parents when they return.

Bedwetting

A child may wet the bed if he is worried or feels insecure. Don't get angry with him. Reassure him, clean and pat him dry, and change his pajamas and the sheets. Settle him calmly back in bed, and let his parents know when they get home.

Sleepwalking

The parents should let you know if a child is likely to sleepwalk. Make sure any stair gates are closed after you have put him to bed. If he does sleepwalk, don't wake him, but guide him gently back to bed. Tell his parents when they come home.

GAMES AND ACTIVITIES

ENTERTAINING YOUNG children is as important as changing a diaper. Time will pass enjoyably for everyone if you join in with the children's activities or introduce new ones. These pages will give you ideas for entertaining younger children: be led by what they enjoy doing. You could take along a "magic bag" filled with toys and games to play with. Older children will tell you what they like doing.

0 – 6 MONTHS

Floor-based activities are ideal for babies up to six months old. They enjoy watching and grasping for objects that are hung close to them, and they respond to being close to you. Give babies plenty of smiles, hugs, and eye contact as you play with them. Babies are very sensitive to your mood; if you are relaxed, they will be too.

Lay him on the floor and give him a safe toy to play with

GIVE him large, bright toys to hold and chew.

LET him grasp objects and explore their different shapes and textures.

A BABY will rely on you for a lot of stimulus. Sit her on your lap or rock her gently in a bouncer chair on the floor, and sing songs or nursery rhymes to her.

AT six months old a baby will be starting to sit up, but he will still need to be supported. Prop him up and surround him with cushions or with pillows to protect him if he falls.

BABIES respond to bright colors and different sounds. Toy keys or rattles are ideal.

6 MONTHS – 1 YEAR

etween six months and a year, babies
ill learn to crawl and then to pull
emselves up into a standing position,
sing people or furniture for support.
hey generally take their first steps
hen they are holding on to furniture,
olding an adult's hand, or pushing
toy cart. They can also understand
asic instructions and will recognize
miliar objects, pictures, and faces.

PUT some blocks or toys
in a box. Show the baby
how to fill and empty
the basket, and praise
him when he does
it himself.

Brightly colored
blocks are ideal

GIVE him some objects that
he can bang together on
the floor – a wooden spoon
and a pan or two pan
lids are excellent.

SELECT rattles
and toys that
the baby will enjoy looking
at, handling, shaking,
dropping, and chewing.

LOOK at board books and
talk about the pictures,
the story, the colors, and
the characters. Let the
baby help you turn
the pages.

HIDE your face behind a
cushion and play "peek-a-boo."

PUT on some music or sing a
song to the baby. Clap in
time to the music.

SHOW the baby his reflection
in a mirror.

ENCOURAGE the baby to copy
you by waving, or pointing
to parts of your body. She
may be able to point to her
nose, mouth, eyes, and ears.

SIT on the floor together and
roll a soft ball around.

CRAWL on the
floor with him
and play with a
push-along toy.

IMPROVISED TOYS

■ Take empty boxes (with
no staples) and some shiny
objects (too large for the
baby to swallow) with you
for the baby to play with.

■ Bring along some old
magazines (not newspapers)
for the baby to scrunch up.
Remove any staples and
don't let her chew paper.

■ Collect fabric scraps of
different patterns, colors,
and textures for her to
feel and explore.

1 YEAR – 18 MONTHS

Children of this age are either crawling or walking, and they want to investigate everything, to pull and push things, and to open and close them. They have no sense of danger, so you must stay close by at all times. Although they will be occupied by activities for short periods of time, their attention span is limited and you are still an essential playmate.

HELP the child discover different sounds by pressing buttons on musical toys or books.

HIDE a toy under a blanket. Make sure she sees where you put it, and look for it together. She will enjoy finding it over and over again.

ENCOURAGE the child to stack building blocks on top of each other and to push the stack of blocks over.

SHOW the child how to play with the shape sorter. Talk about their size and color, and praise her when she puts them in correctly.

LOOK at models or pictures of animals together, and imitate the noises that the animals make.

LET the child scribble on paper. Give her large non-toxic crayons that are easy to hold and remember to protect the floor or table. Make sure she doesn't put the crayons in her mouth.

PUSH a toy backward and forward to each other.

SHE will enjoy playing with a push-along toy, such as a shopping cart. Make sure you keep an eye on her in case she loses her balance.

LOOK at picture books together. Encourage the child to join in by pointing to the illustrations and describing what you can see

SING nursery rhymes and activity songs to her, or play her a familiar tape.

PLAY hide and seek in one room, but stay in sight.

IMPROVISED TOYS

Take along a box filled with objects in a variety of colors and textures. Make sure the objects are too large to swallow and have no sharp edges.

18 MONTHS – 3 YEARS

Children develop rapidly and become more independent during this time. They gain greater control of their hands and bodies, and their use of language becomes more skilled. Frustrations and fears can influence their emotions and behavior, and you may have to deal with tantrums (see page 32); distract or divert them, and give them lots of praise.

IMPROVISED TOYS

▓ Drape a towel over a chair to make a house for toys or a hideaway den.

▓ Make paper boats or hats, or fold and cut paper to make cut-out shapes.

▓ Play sorting, ordering, and matching games with socks or containers.

GIVE the child a brush or cloth and pretend to clean together. He will like following you around and imitating what you do.

HOLD a pretend tea party and invite all her stuffed toys. She will enjoy making tea for them.

CHOOSE a jigsaw puzzle with large, colorful pieces and do it together.

DO some painting together, but check with the parents first and ask where to do it. Make sure the child wears an apron to protect his clothes.

PLAY hide-and-seek behind the curtain or chair. Stay in one room.

PUT on familiar songs and sing along to them with her. You could also do actions for her to copy.

ENCOURAGE him to play with construction toys that can be easily pieced together.

SHOW the child simple storybooks with plenty of pictures and repetition. Talk about the pictures.

IF there is a VCR, sit and watch her favorite programs with her. Check with her parents first.

THREAD very large wooden beads onto a shoelace or piece of string to make a snake.

GIVE him nontoxic modeling dough, but protect the carpet.

4 – 5 YEARS

By the age of four, children show a real curiosity about the world. They will ask you questions and want to show off their skills, like hopping or skipping. They have a longer attention span, so they can occupy themselves for short periods of time, although they will rely on you for some suggestions. Ask the parents what they would like you to do with the children and where.

IMPROVISED TOYS

■ You can make a simple mask by drawing a face on a paper plate, cutting out the eyes, and taping it to a wooden spoon.

■ Take along boxes, pots, nontoxic glue, and a spreader to make toys. Ask parents where to make them.

PLAY "I spy." You can use either colors or letter sounds for clues.

SHOW him how to thread beads and other objects onto string or yarn to make ornaments.

ENCOURAGE the child to listen and dance to music.

GET out the building blocks. Ask him to show you how high he can build a tower.

TAKE along some old clothes for her to dress up in.

GIVE him old magazines to cut out pictures from, using rounded scissors. Stick them onto paper using nontoxic glue.

READ to her, play story tapes, or make up stories – ask her to guess what happens next.

PLAY simple games that involve throwing dice and moving pieces.

PUT down newspaper and do some finger painting. Check with the parents first and ask them where to do it. Make sure he wears an apron.

6 – 8 YEARS

Children at school show an increasing interest in reading, writing, and simple math, and may want to continue with these activities at home, although they might be tired in the evenings. They want to know how everything works, and like to become involved in "grown-up" activities. They are independent enough to do most simple tasks alone, such as dressing, undressing, and going to the bathroom, but they might ask for help if they are tired.

READ a story to the child. She may want to read to you, or even make up her own stories. You could also write down some difficult words for her to copy.

CHOOSE easy number and word puzzles for her to solve.

PLAY word games such as "I spy."

SUPERVISE cutting, sticking, and painting activities.

LET the child help you with simple food preparation, such as making sandwiches or evening snacks.

YOU could practice the fire escape plan together with older children so they are familiar with it (see page 50).

IMPROVISED TOYS

■ Collect empty egg cartons or toilet rolls to use for junk modeling.

■ Make puppets out of paper bags: draw a face on the bag and twist the corners to make ears. Fill the bag with paper and tie the bottom around a stick.

■ You can make hand puppets out of old socks or mittens: stick or sew on buttons for eyes, and strands of yarn for hair.

SUGGEST playing board or card games. Try to let her win; she may get upset if she loses.

PUT on story tapes for her to listen to – you can borrow new ones from the library.

GIVE her a pen and paper to practice writing or drawing.

BROTHERS AND SISTERS

Babysitting for children of different ages means coping with different needs and demands all at the same time. Many children will be able to entertain themselves for periods of time on their own, but sometimes, just as one child has settled down and is playing with a toy, the other child will want it too. You will be able to reason with older brothers and sisters and explain sharing and taking turns. With children under four, you'll find it easier to distract them with something different or exciting.

ALLOW children to take on different roles with each other through pretend games such as playing with dolls.

STAY close at hand, even if children are getting along well together. Tantrums flare up quickly and you may need to act as referee.

INVOLVE older children in playing games with younger children. Perhaps they can show them some pictures, or help them to balance building blocks.

ARGUMENTS

▨ If a child has a tantrum, let him get over it on his own, but stay in the same room (see page 32).

▨ Brothers and sisters can rebel against you if you introduce rules that they are not used to. Be clear about your expectations and stick to what you say.

DISTRACT a child with a different activity if she intrudes on her sister's game.

MOST children enjoy making cards, pictures, and presents for special people such as their grandparents or parents. Let them each make a card.

ENCOURAGE an older child to read a story to her younger brother or sister.

HOME SAFETY
AND
FIRST AID

As a babysitter you need to know what
you can do to prevent emergencies and how to
deal with them if they do occur. You also need to
know what to do if a child becomes ill while you
are babysitting. Read and study this section
carefully, although it is no substitute for the
practical training of a first aid course.

HOME SAFETY

I T IS IMPORTANT to think about home safety and accident prevention before you babysit for a family and during the time you are in the home. Considering how you would deal with various situations will increase your confidence and the children's and your safety.

FINDING YOUR WAY AROUND THE HOME

As a babysitter, it is essential that you know where to find baby equipment, children's toys or clothing, kitchen utensils, and the first aid kit, if there is one. You will also need to ask parents about the home itself.

• Find out where light switches are positioned and where a flashlight is kept in case of a power outage.

• Ask where the telephone is, if there is one. Make sure the parents have left contact numbers, a neighbor's address, and directions to the home, close to the telephone in case of an emergency.

• Find out where the circuit breaker and the water shutoff are.

• Make sure you understand any other instructions before the parents leave.

KEEPING THE HOME SAFE

Ask if you need to lock the windows or doors and find out where the keys are kept. Lock the front door and check that the windows are closed. Close any safety gates securely.

Safety gates
Shut any safety gates in doorways or on the stairs.

ANSWERING THE DOOR

If someone comes to the door, don't open it unless there is a safety chain in place. If there is no chain, speak to the visitor through a window or the closed door. Don't allow anyone in, whoever they say they are; don't admit a divorce parent before calling to check with the resident parent. If you see anyone acting suspiciously outside, call the police.

ANSWERING THE TELEPHONE

If the telephone rings, just say "hello." Tell the caller you are a family friend and offer to take a message. Don't say that the parents are out or you are baby sitting. If there is an answering machine leave it on, but listen to the message. If you have threatening or strange calls, ca the parents, your parents, or the police

PREVENTING INJURIES

t is the parents' responsibility to make
heir house safe, but there are some
azards that you can help a child avoid.
upervise babies, toddlers, and young
hildren all the time. If you have to
nswer the door or use the
hone, take them with you.
ou should also be aware of where
lder children are and what they are
oing. Remove any obvious hazards,
ach as toys left in doorways that
ou or the children could trip over.

Playing alone
*Be aware of what
children are doing.*

KITCHEN

here are several hazards for young
hildren in the kitchen. It is also the
oom where you may be most distracted
you are preparing food or drinks.

ligh chairs
Always strap a baby into her high
hair using the safety belt.

Don't put the chair
here a baby can
each out and pull
nings down.

lways use the
afety belt

*igh chair
afety
ever leave a
ild on her own
a high chair.*

abinets and drawers
lake sure you shut all cabinets and
rawers properly. Many parents attach
fety locks to drawers containing
issors or knives, or to cabinets that
ntain alcohol, medicine, or chemicals.

Floors
• Remove toys from the floor before
you cook, and always wipe up any
liquid you have spilled.

• If there is a playpen, make sure you
use it.

Drinks
• Never carry a baby while you are
preparing his bottle – steam or boiling
water from the pot could scald him.

• Don't make a hot drink if there is
a toddler or baby at your feet.

• Don't sit a child on the work surface –
she could fall off or grab something.

Cooking
• Keep children away from cooking
activities. Use the back burners and turn
pan handles away from the stove edge.

• Put matches out of reach.

• Oven doors become very hot. Keep
young children away from the oven,
and be particularly careful with
crawling babies who may press their
hands on the oven door for support.

LIVING ROOM

You will probably spend most of your time with the children in the living room, so look out for potential hazards.

Television, VCR, and stereo system
• Don't let children touch any electrical equipment.

• Check that wires are tucked away and always replace safety socket covers.

Fires and heaters
• Keep children away from gas fires, hot radiators, and electric heaters.

• Use a fire screen if there is an open fire and don't light a fire yourself. *Never* leave a child alone in a room where there is a lighted fire. Keep matches out of reach.

Floor and surfaces
Don't leave any potential hazards, such as scissors, glasses, or mugs, on the floor or on surfaces that are within a child's reach. Remember that a child could receive a serious cut if she falls on a cup or glass, or she could be scalded by a spilled hot drink.

Toys
• Put any toys that have small pieces out of reach of children under three.

• Clear the floor of any toys that the children have finished playing with so that no one falls or trips over them.

• Encourage the children to help you pick up the toys and put them away.

BATHROOM

Parents should prepare children for bed before you arrive, but you may need to supervise hand- and face-washing, and teeth-brushing. You may occasionally be asked to bathe younger children. Don't let a child lock himself in the bathroom.

Sinks
Make sure the water from the tap is not too hot and check the temperature of the water in the sink. Don't let children put the plug in the sink and leave the tap running.

BATHS

▧ Run cold water before hot and always check the temperature before children get into the bath. Use a nonslip mat if possible.

▧ *Never* leave a baby or young child alone in the bath, even for a minute. A baby can drown in just 1in (2.5cm) of water.

Toilets and potties
Always go with a young child when she needs to use the toilet. Help her put the toilet seat in place – she may use a step. If she uses a potty, flush away the contents and rinse it well.

Help her undo and do up awkward buttons and zippers

Surfaces and cabinets
Mop up any spills on the floor and check that cabinets with safety catches are shut properly. Put other hazards, such as scissors or razors, out of reach.

48

HALL AND STAIRS

Stairs are an obvious hazard for young children. Supervise them going up and down the stairs and check that they hold on to the handrail. If you are carrying a baby on the stairs, always hold on to the handrail.

Safety on stairs
Encourage young children to crawl backward down the stairs.

• Keep any stair gates shut, even after the children have gone to bed, and leave a light on in the hall so that you can see to check the children. They may wake up during the evening and want to come downstairs; some children even sleepwalk occasionally.

• Remove any toys that are lying around on the stairs or landing, or in the hall, so that neither you nor the children trip over them.

BEDROOM

Either keep windows shut or check that children cannot climb up and fall from an open window.

If the children have bunk beds, don't let them fool around on the top bunk in case they fall off.

Pick up toys from the floor so that you don't fall on them in the dark if you have to attend to the children.

Baby monitors
If there is a monitor, turn the transmitter on in the baby's room and keep the receiver with you.

Make sure that the monitor is turned up enough for you to hear the baby.

Cribs
Put a young baby to sleep on his back or side, *never* on his front. Check that he doesn't get too hot or too cold.

Check that the crib sides are up and don't leave any stuffed toys near a young baby's head.

Quiet check
Look in quietly on sleeping babies every half hour and on children about once an hour.

• An older baby will move himself into a more comfortable position and will probably want to sleep with his favorite stuffed toy.

FIRE: EMERGENCY PROCEDURES

As you familiarize yourself with the home, think about what you would do if a fire were to break out while you were babysitting. Consider how you would escape a fire upstairs, downstairs, or at the front or back of the home. Ask if the parents have a fire escape plan and, if not, that they prepare one. If the windows are locked, make sure the keys are nearby. Ask the parents whether they have a fire blanket or extinguisher and to show you how to use it. Find out if there are smoke alarms in the home.

If a fire breaks out

Investigate immediately if you see or smell smoke, but never open the door to a room where you think a fire might have started unless the children are in that room. Don't try to put out a fire yourself. Instead, get the children and leave the building immediately, closing all the doors behind you. Don't go back inside; go to a neighbor's home, and call the fire department and the parents.

CLOTHING ON FIRE

▦ If your clothing catches fire, stop, drop to the floor, and roll.

▦ If a child's clothes catch fire, don't let him run around. Wrap him tightly in a blanket or coat. Lay him on the ground and tell him to roll to put out the flames.

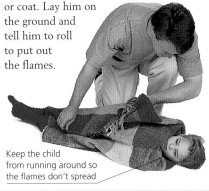

Keep the child from running around so the flames don't spread

Stove fire

If anything on the stove catches fire, turn off the stove or burners. Smother the flames with a fire blanket, a wet dish towel, or a wet hand-towel, and leave it there. Never throw water on the flames.

TRAPPED IN A ROOM

Put a rolled-up blanket at the base of the door

▦ If you are trapped in a room, close the door and put blankets, rugs, or clothing against the bottom to keep the smoke out.

▦ Go to a window, open it, and shout loudly for help.

▦ Keep yourself and the children low, where the air is clearest.

▦ If you have to escape through the window, help the children out first. Each child should slide out, hang on to you, then drop to the ground.

▦ If you have to break glass, put a blanket over any broken edges before escaping.

CARING FOR A SICK CHILD

TAKING A TEMPERATURE

If a child becomes ill while you are babysitting, call her parents and, if possible, take her temperature (see right). If it is above 99.6° F (37.5° C), she has a fever (see page 52). If it is above 104° F (40° C), it can be dangerous, and may trigger convulsions in young children (see page 65). Cool the child with a damp sponge and call her doctor.

FOR A CHILD

A digital thermometer is accurate and easy to use. Put it under the child's arm and take a reading when it beeps.

FOR A BABY

Use a heat-sensitive strip that changes color according to the baby's temperature. Hold it across the forehead by both ends for one minute, or until one color is constant. Or use a digital thermometer under the arm (see above).

TAKING A PULSE

After taking the child's temperature, make her comfortable and take her pulse. Make a note of the pulse rate, its strength, and the time you took it.

FOR A BABY

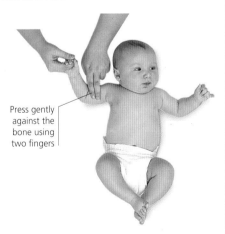

Press gently against the bone using two fingers

FOR A CHILD

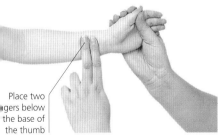

Place two fingers below the base of the thumb

Feel for the wrist pulse. Place two fingers against the wrist, just below the base of the thumb. Count the number of beats in one minute or 15 seconds and multiply by four. A normal rate is about 90 beats per minute.

Feel the pulse by placing two fingers on the inside of the arm, between the shoulder and elbow. Count the number of beats in one minute or 15 seconds and multiply by four. A normal rate is about 120 beats per minute.

Childhood Illnesses

Illness	What can I do ?	
FEVER	▦ If a child feels ill or her skin is flushed or hot, take her temperature (see page 51). ▦ If it is over 104°F (40°C), call her doctor and parents, and sponge her with tepid water.	▦ If her temperature is above 99.6°F (37.5°C), lay her down on a bed or sofa, but do not cover her. Give her water or diluted fruit juice to drink, and call her parents.
VOMITING	▦ Hold the child over a bowl and support her while she is sick. Wipe her face with a cloth wrung out in lukewarm water. ▦ Let her rest, and put a bowl and a fresh drink by her bed.	▦ Encourage her to drink small amounts of cool water. ▦ If she is repeatedly sick, call her doctor and parents.
DIARRHEA	▦ Give babies cooled, boiled water – not milk. ▦ Give an older child cool fluids to drink, e.g. add a pinch of salt and a little sugar to cool water or diluted orange juice.	▦ Ask the child to drink slowly and often. ▦ If the diarrhea continues, or the child is vomiting or has a fever, call her doctor and parents.
RASH	▦ Rashes in young children are very common and may be caused by an allergy or virus. If the child feels well, tell the parents when they get home.	▦ If the child is feverish, take her temperature (see page 51 and "fever," above) and call her doctor and parents.
FEELING FAINT	▦ Get the child to lie down. Raise her legs on pillows so that they are above her heart level. Tell the child to take deep breaths. ▦ Loosen any tight clothing. ▦ Open a nearby window or gently fan the child's face.	▦ When the child is feeling better, help her to sit up slowly. Call her parents. ▦ If she does not regain consciousness quickly after fainting, see page 74.

ACHES AND PAINS

WHAT CAN I DO?

Children often develop aches and pains that may be a sign of illness or a result of anxiety. Make the child comfortable and if the pain continues, call her doctor and parents.

Prop her up with pillows

STOMACHACHE

1 Encourage the child to sit or lie against some pillows or cushions so she is comfortable. Keep a bowl nearby if she feels sick.

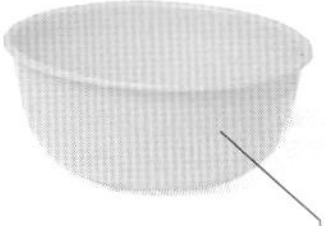

2 Don't give the child anything to eat or drink while she still has pain in her stomach, except a little water to moisten her lips.

IF *the pain is severe or does not ease after 30 minutes, call her doctor and parents.*

Put a bowl near her if she feels sick

EARACHE

1 Make the child comfortable, sitting or lying against pillows. Fill a hot-water bottle, cover it with a towel, and let her put it against her sore ear.

2 If the pain is severe, or if there is a discharge, a fever, or a loss of hearing, call her doctor as well.

Lay her against pillows

TOOTHACHE

1 Encourage the child to lie down with her sore tooth against a pillow.

2 Fill a hot-water bottle with warm water, cover it with a towel, and place it gently under the child's jaw. Call her parents and ask them what you should do.

IF *the jaw is swollen and the pain is severe, call her doctor as well.*

BASICS OF FIRST AID

THE FOLLOWING pages show you what to do if an emergency occurs. Although such emergencies are rare, it is important to be as prepared as possible. There is no substitute for proper first aid training. If you have not taken a first aid course, consider taking one soon.

WHAT TO DO IN AN EMERGENCY

1 Assess the Situation
Keep calm and try to discover what happened, who is injured, if there is any danger to yourself or the injured person, and whether you need to call 911 or the local EMS (Emergency Medical Services).

2 Think of Safety
Do not put yourself at risk of injury – you won't be able to help a child if you are hurt. Remove any source of danger from the child and only move the child if it is absolutely necessary – make sure you do this very carefully.

3 Treat Serious Conditions First
Unconsciousness (see pages 70 to 78), severe bleeding (see page 62), and severe burns (see page 60) are life-threatening conditions. If more than one child is injured, go to the quiet child first – he may be unconscious.

4 Get Help
Dial 911 or your local EMS, and give the following information:
- the telephone number
- the address, and directions to the home
- the type of emergency
- who is hurt, and how he is injured.

Don't hang up the telephone until you are told to do so by the dispatcher.

Telephone the parents when you have given first aid and tell them what has happened. If you cannot contact the parents, call an alternative contact number that they have left you. If you accompany a child to the hospital, you will need someone to stay at home with any other children.

> **IF** *there is no telephone, the parents should leave you the address of the nearest neighbor who is in, has a telephone, and who will be able to help in an emergency.*

FIRST AID KIT

there is a first aid kit in the home, it should be
ccessible and easy to identify. A well-stocked kit
nould contain the articles below, and it may also
ontain other items, such as disposable gloves.
Iedicine should not be kept in the first aid kit.

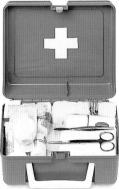

First aid kit

DRESSINGS

dhesive bandages are used
or minor wounds. Choose
ne that is the right size and
ape. Larger sterile dressings
re for more serious wounds.

Adhesive
bandages

Gauze pads

Eye pad with bandage

Scissors

Tweezers

Sterile nonadhesive pad

Sterile dressing with bandage

Hypoallergenic tape

BANDAGES

These are used to secure
dressings and support injured
joints. Conforming bandages
are easy to use and they shape
themselves to the contours of
the body. Triangular bandages
are mostly used as slings.

Small conforming
bandage

Large conforming
bandage

Crepe roller
bandage with
securing clip

Safety pins

Folded triangular bandage

Large crepe roller bandage

55

NOSEBLEEDS

WHAT CAN I DO?

WHAT DO I NEED?

- Bowl or basin
- Tissues or cotton balls
- Lukewarm water
- Towel

1 Sit the child down with his head bent forward. Ask him to breathe through his mouth. Pinch the fleshy part of his nose.

Get him to tilt his head well forward

Comfort him and ask him to breathe through his mouth

2 Hold his nostrils together for about 10 minutes. Tell him to spit out any fluid in his mouth.

3 Release the pressure. If the bleeding has not stopped, pinch the nose for another 10 minutes.

Pinch his nostrils together for 10 minutes

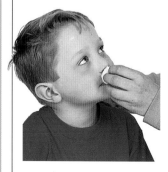

4 Once the bleeding has stopped, gently wash the area around the nose with tissues or a cotton ball dipped in warm water.

Let him spit or dribble into a bowl

5 Dry with a towel. Sit quietly together for at least 30 minutes. Don't let him blow his nose.

IF *the nosebleed goes on for longer than half an hour, call his doctor and parents.*

CUTS AND ABRASIONS

WHAT CAN I DO?

1 Reassure the child with a hug and sit her down. Get the first aid kit. If the child is young, take her with you and find the first aid items you need together.

WHAT DO I NEED?

- Warm water
- Gauze pads/washcloth
- Adhesive bandage or dressing (check for allergy)

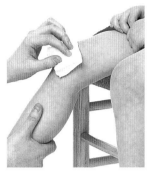

3 Pat the area dry with clean gauze and apply pressure to stop the bleeding. Do not use cotton balls.

Wipe the abrasion gently with gauze pads or a washcloth

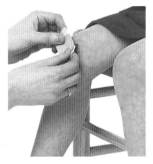

4 Check for allergy to adhesive bandages (see page 87). Cover the cut with a bandage, or nonadhesive dressing, that has a pad large enough to cover the abrasion.

2 Use gauze pads or a washcloth soaked in warm water to wash the abrasion. Remove any loose particles of dirt or gravel. Use a clean gauze pad for each wipe and wipe away from the wound.

IF *there is anything embedded in the cut, do not try to remove it. See page 63.*

REMOVING SPLINTERS

WHAT CAN I DO?

WHAT DO I NEED?

- Soap and warm water
- Sterile tweezers
- Adhesive bandage

1 Clean the area around a splinter with soap and warm water. If it is deeply embedded, barbed, near the eye or over a joint, treat as an embedded object (see page 63).

Pull a splinter straight out at the angle it went in

2 Grasp the splinter as close to the skin as possible and draw it out.

3 Squeeze the wound so it bleeds. Wash and dry the area. Cover with an adhesive bandage, or a nonadhesive dressing. If it is hard to take out, stop, and tell the parents.

FOREIGN BODIES

WHAT CAN I DO?

IN THE EAR

If something is stuck in a child's ear, don't try to remove it. Call her doctor and parents.

INSECT IN EAR

1 Sit her down. Hold her head, with the affected ear upwards.

2 Pour some lukewarm water into the affected ear so the insect floats out.

IN THE EYE

Encourage the child to keep blinking and encourage her to lift her upper eyelid over her lower one. If the foreign body doesn't dislodge itself, call her doctor and parents.

IN THE NOSE

If a child puts something up her nose, tell her to breathe through her mouth. Call her doctor and parents.

STINGS

WHAT CAN I DO?

WHAT DO I NEED?

- Plastic/credit card
- Cloth and cold water

1 Scrape the stinger and poison sac from the skin with the thin edge of a credit card. Don't squeeze the stinger or sac.

2 Cool the area with a bag of ice in a towel or cloth wrung out in cool water.

STING IN MOUTH

If a child is stung in the mouth, it may swell. Give her cold water to drink or an ice cube to suck. Call 911 or the local EMS and her parents.

IF *she collapses after a sting, or has breathing difficulties, call 911 or the local EMS and her parents immediately.*

POISONING

WHAT CAN I DO?

A child can be poisoned by drinking household chemicals, such as bleach, or by drinking alcohol, or eating pills or berries.

1 Talk calmly to the child; try to find out what he has taken, when he took it, and how much. Don't try to make him sick. Remove any contaminated clothing.

2 Call at once the Poison Information Center and his parents. Let him rest; watch him until help arrives.

IF *the child becomes unconscious, see page 74.*

BURNS AND SCALDS

WHAT CAN I DO?

WHAT DO I NEED?

▓ Cold water
▓ Scissors
▓ Clean sheet/pillowcase
or a dressing

1 Cool the burn or scald
immediately with cool
water for at least ten
minutes. If the burn was
caused by a chemical, wash
it all off first by holding the
affected area under cool,
running water for ten to
15 minutes.

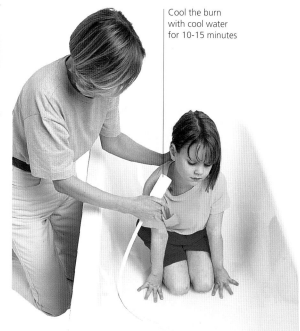

Cool the burn
with cool water
for 10-15 minutes

Take off her
clothing when the
burn has cooled
and cool again

2 Remove the child's
clothing once the
burn has cooled. Cut
around any material
stuck to the skin. Cool
the burn again. Don't
apply cream to the burn.

3 Cover the burn loosely
with a dressing or a clean,
nonfluffy material. Call 911
or the local EMS if the burn
is severe, and contact the
child's parents.

A pillowcase makes
a good bandage

IF *she has burns on her
mouth or throat, watch
her breathing, loosen the
clothing around her neck,
and give her cool water to
sip. Call 911 or the local
EMS and her parents.*

IF *the burn is severe or
the child shows signs
of shock, see "shock"
(page 63). If she becomes
unconscious, see page 74.*

HEAD AND FACIAL INJURIES

WHAT CAN I DO?

SCALP WOUND

Hold a clean pad to the wound

Bandage the pad in place

WHAT DO I NEED?

▦ Clean pad
▦ Bandage

1 Scalp wounds can bleed heavily, so hold a thick pad to the wound. Place another pad on top, if necessary. Avoid pressing the wound directly, in case the skull is fractured.

2 Bandage the dressing in place, but make sure that it is not too tight.

3 Help the child to lie down with her head and shoulders propped up. Call her parents, and stay with her until they arrive.

IF *you suspect her head or neck has been injured, prevent any movement with pillows to each side. See page 74 and call 911 or the local EMS.*

BROKEN NOSE, CHEEKBONE, AND JAW

If a child has injured her nose or cheekbone, sit her down and hold a cloth wrung out in cool water against the injury to reduce swelling. Call 911 or the local EMS and her parents. If her nose is bleeding, see page 56.

Hold a cool, damp cloth against her cheek

If her jaw is injured, hold a soft pad under her jaw and support the jaw with your hand. Call 911 or the local EMS and her parents.

IF *the child becomes unconscious, see page 74.*

SEVERE BLEEDING

WHAT CAN I DO?

Press firmly on
the wound and
elevate the
injured part

WHAT DO I NEED?

- Clean pad
- Blanket/towel
- Sterile dressing, bandage

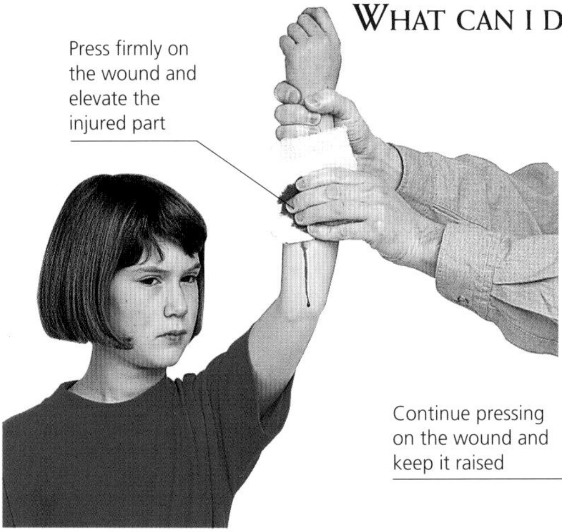

Continue pressing
on the wound and
keep it raised

1 Press a clean pad firmly over the wound to stop the bleeding. Raise the injured part above the level of the child's heart.

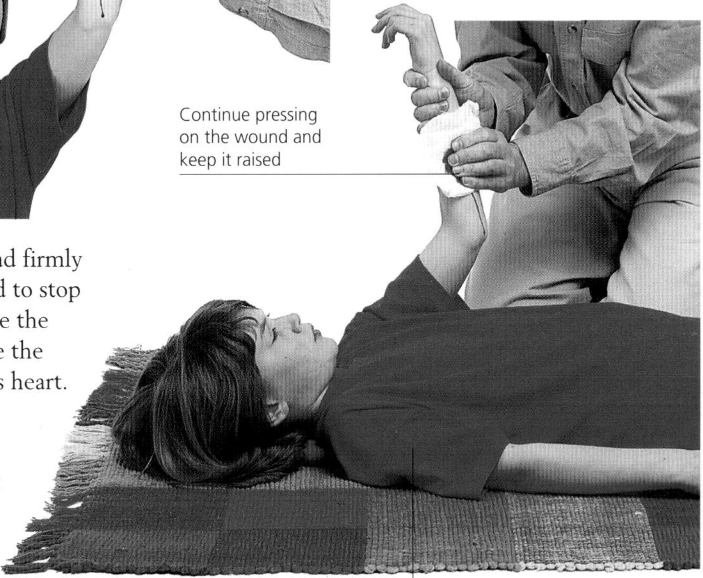

2 Lay the child down and put a towel or thin blanket under her head. Keep her legs raised about 12in (30cm). Keep the injured part raised and press on the wound until the bleeding is controlled.

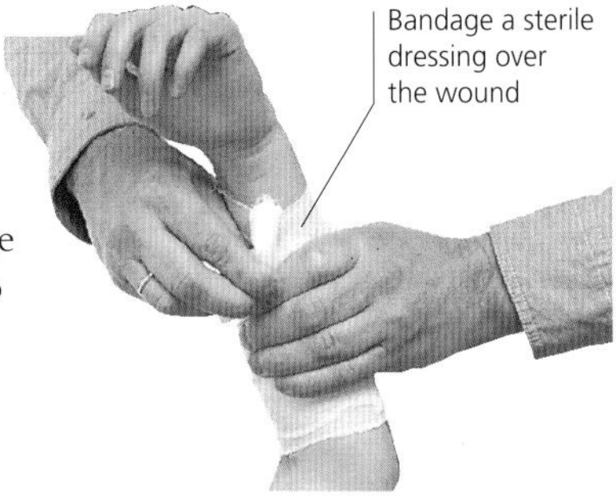

Lay the child
down and keep
her legs raised

3 Cover the injury with a sterile dressing that is larger than the wound. Bandage it in place and keep the injury raised.

Bandage a sterile
dressing over
the wound

4 The bandage should be firm, but not too tight. If blood is still coming through, bandage another pad on top. Call 911 or the local EMS and her parents, and if bleeding continues, follow the first aid for shock (see opposite).

SHOCK

WHAT CAN I DO?

Recognizing shock

- *Follows injuries such as bleeding or burns*
- *Pale, cold, sweaty skin*
- *Fast pulse, getting weaker*
- *Fast, shallow breathing*

Keep the injury raised

Keep her head low

Raise her legs about 12in (30cm) and support them

1 If the child shows any signs of shock, continue treating the injury and lay her down with her legs raised about 12in (30cm), using pillows for support.

2 Loosen any tight clothing and cover her with a blanket.

3 Call 911 or the local EMS and her parents. If she is thirsty, moisten her lips, but don't let her drink or eat.

IF *the child becomes unconscious, see page 74.*

EMBEDDED OBJECT IN WOUND

WHAT CAN I DO?

1 Do not try to remove any object stuck in a wound. Call 911 or the local EMS and contact the child's parents.

Raise the injured part

Press around the object in the wound

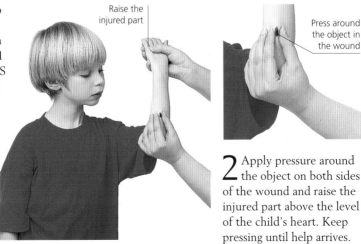

2 Apply pressure around the object on both sides of the wound and raise the injured part above the level of the child's heart. Keep pressing until help arrives.

FRACTURES AND SPRAINS

WHAT CAN I DO?

WHAT DO I NEED?

▓ Padding
▓ Cold compress

Make injury
comfortable
with padding

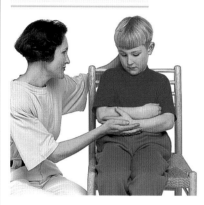

1 Sit the child down and raise and support the injury. If he is in too much pain to sit down, let him find his most comfortable position.

2 Place padding around the injured part to keep it still and make it comfortable. Let him support the injury himself. If you suspect a leg fracture, hold onto his feet.

3 To keep down any swelling, apply a washcloth or towel wrung out in cool water. You can also use a bag of ice or frozen vegetables covered with a towel or cloth. Don't apply cold to an open wound.

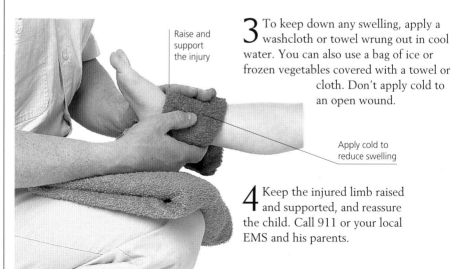

Raise and
support
the injury

Apply cold to
reduce swelling

4 Keep the injured limb raised and supported, and reassure the child. Call 911 or your local EMS and his parents.

SEIZURES AND CONVULSIONS

WHAT CAN I DO?

FEVER CONVULSIONS

Recognizing fever convulsions

- *These are seizures that may develop in a child under four with a high temperature or infection*
- *May have stiff, arching back and clenched fists*
- *Face may look blue, if he is holding his breath*
- *May be flushed and sweating, with hot forehead*

Remove his clothes to cool him down

1 Undress the child down to his diaper or underwear. Clear a space around him to protect him from injury.

2 Cool him by sponging him with lukewarm water. Start at his head and work down his body.

Sponge him with tepid water

3 When he is cooled, the convulsions will stop. Roll him onto his side and cover him with a sheet. Call his doctor and parents.

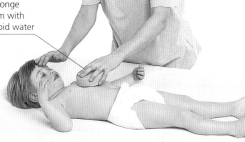

EPILEPTIC CONVULSIONS

Recognizing epileptic convulsions

- *Child falls unconscious and face may be blue*
- *Rigid, jerky movement, arched back, or fists*
- *Froth or bubbles around the mouth*

Clear a space around her and don't hold her down

1 If the child starts to fall, try to catch her and help her down. Clear a space around her so she doesn't hurt herself. Loosen any tight clothes.

2 Put soft padding, but not a pillow, under her head. Don't hold her down or give her anything to eat or drink.

3 When the convulsions are over, call her parents, and 911 or the local EMS if this is the first time she has had convulsions. If she is still unconscious, see page 74. She may want to sleep.

65

BREATHING DIFFICULTIES

WHAT CAN I DO?

ASTHMA

Recognizing asthma

- *Coughing and wheezing*
- *Distress and anxiety*
- *Bluish tinge to face or lips*

1 Help the child relax. Sit her down, leaning forward. An older child will find her most comfortable position.

2 If she has medication for asthma, such as an inhaler, let her use it.

IF *this is her first attack, call her doctor and parents. If it is severe, or does not ease with medication, call 911 or the local EMS.*

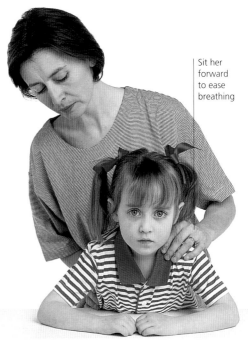

Sit her forward to ease breathing

CROUP

Recognizing croup

- *Difficulty breathing in*
- *Short, barking cough*
- *Blue-tinged skin*

1 Help the child sit up and prop him up with pillows. Boil a kettle or run hot water to make a steamy atmosphere.

2 Bring the child into the steamy atmosphere and help him relax so that he breathes in the steam. Call his doctor and parents if you are concerned.

66

CHOKING: BABY

WHAT CAN I DO?

Recognizing choking

- *Breathing obstructed*
- *Face may turn blue*
- *May make strange noises or no sound*

Give five sharp blows on his back

1 Lay the baby along your forearm. Support his chin. Give five sharp blows on his back.

2 If the blockage does not clear, turn him face-up on your other arm. Put two fingers low on his breastbone and give him five chest thrusts.

Use two fingers only

3 Check the baby to see if the back blows and chest thrusts have cleared the obstruction. If they have, call the baby's doctor and parents. If there is still a blockage, call 911 or the local EMS.

4 Repeat the first two steps until the blockage has cleared or help arrives.

IF *the baby becomes unconscious, see page 70.*

CHOKING: CONSCIOUS CHILD

WHAT CAN I DO?

Recognizing choking

- *Clutching of throat*
- *Face may turn blue*
- *Child unable to speak or breathe*

3 Grasp your fist with your other hand and press into her abdomen with a quick upward thrust.

Give a quick upward thrust

1 If the child starts to choke, tell her to cough. If the blockage doesn't clear immediately, go on to step 2.

2 Stand or kneel behind her. Wrap your arms around her abdomen just above the line of the hips. Make a fist with one hand and place the thumb side of your fist against the middle of her abdomen, just above her navel.

Position your fist on her abdomen

4 If the blockage hasn't cleared, repeat steps 2 and 3 until the obstruction clears, or until the child becomes unconscious.

IF *the child becomes unconscious, the throat will relax and she may start to breathe. If she doesn't start breathing, see opposite.*

5 When the blockage is clear, make the child comfortable. Call her doctor and her parents.

CHOKING: UNCONSCIOUS CHILD

WHAT CAN I DO?

Follow the procedure below if a choking child falls unconscious. But remember, a child may choke and fall unconscious before you find her, and the cause may not be obvious.

1 Check the child for signs of consciousness and breathing (see pages 74–5). Try giving artificial respiration (see page 77, steps 1 to 4); if this fails, try again. Call 911 or the local EMS.

Tilt her head to clear the airway

2 Lay the child on her back. Kneel across her, straddling her legs. Put the heel of one hand just above her navel and place the heel of the other hand on top. Give five abdominal thrusts.

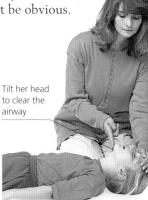

Thrust upward and inward each time

Put the heel of one hand above the other

3 Open the airway by lifting the child's lower jaw and tongue. Only if you can see the object, sweep her mouth with a finger to remove it.

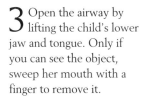

Pinch the child's nostrils closed

4 Tilt the child's head and give a breath of artificial respiration again (see page 77, steps 1 to 3). Watch to see if air is making the chest rise. If this does not happen, tilt the head again and try another breath.

5 If you cannot get air into her lungs, repeat steps 2 to 4, starting with abdominal thrusts, until help arrives or the blockage has cleared. Call the parents once help arrives.

UNCONSCIOUS BABY

If a baby (under one year old) is not responding to you and you cannot wake him, he may be unconscious. You will need to assess his condition immediately by following the procedure below.

ASSESS THE BABY'S CONDITION

Check the baby's responses

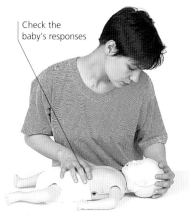

Listen for breaths and look for chest movements

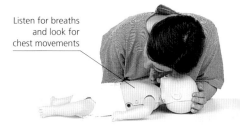

3 Put your ear by his mouth and nose for 3–5 seconds to listen for breaths and feel for breath on your cheek. Watch his chest and abdomen to see if they're moving. If he's not breathing, give two slow breaths of artificial respiration (see page 72, steps 1 to 3). If the air does not make his chest rise, give first aid for choking (see page 67) before going to step 4.

1 Try rousing the baby by calling his name and tapping his feet. Don't shake him, in case he has suffered a spinal cord injury.

Tilt his head back slightly – lift his chin

2 If the baby is still unconscious, tilt his head back slightly – this keeps the airway open (see right) and allows air to enter the lungs. Don't tilt his head if you think his neck might be injured.

KEEPING THE AIRWAY CLEAR

Tilting the head slightly brings the tongue away from the back of the throat and opens the passage to the lungs (airway).

Blocked Airway

Tongue fallen back

Blocked airway

Unblocked Airway

Tongue forward

Unblocked airway

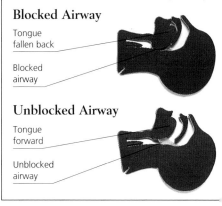

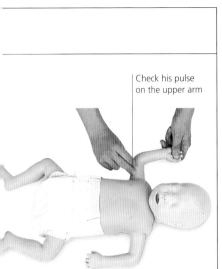

Check his pulse on the upper arm

4 Check the baby's pulse. Put your thumb on the outside of the arm, midway between the shoulder and elbow. Use two fingers to feel for a pulse on the inner side of the arm, pressing toward the bone. Feel for 5-10 seconds before deciding whether the pulse is absent.

5 If the baby is still unconscious, act according to your findings – see below. If the baby regains consciousness, call 911 or the local EMS and his parents. Watch him very carefully until help arrives.

IF *in doubt, always dial 911 or your local EMS for help.*

If the baby is still unconscious, but is breathing and has a pulse, see right.

If the baby is not breathing, but still has a pulse, see page 72.

If the baby is not breathing, and does not have a pulse, see page 73.

BABY BREATHING AND HAS A PULSE

1 Treat any life-threatening injuries, such as severe burns (see page 60) or bleeding (see page 62), before going on to the next step.

Keep his head tilted

2 Cradle the baby in your arms with his head tilted to keep his airway open. Watch him carefully.

3 Take the baby with you to the telephone and call 911 or your local EMS. Then call his parents.

4 Keep the baby in your arms until help arrives. Watch him carefully for any changes in his condition.

BABY NOT BREATHING BUT HAS PULSE

If the baby is not breathing, but has a pulse, you will need to breathe air into his lungs (artificial respiration).

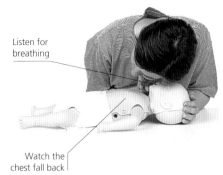

Listen for breathing

Watch the chest fall back

3 Give one slow breath every three seconds. Continue to breathe into the baby's mouth and nose for one minute.

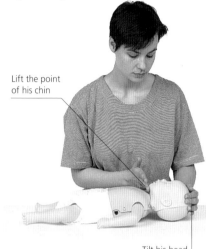

Lift the point of his chin

Tilt his head back slightly

1 Place the baby on his back on a firm surface. Lift the point of his chin and tilt his head back slightly.

Check the pulse in his arm

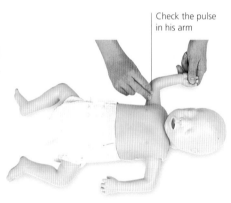

4 Stop and check the pulse (see page 71, step 4). If there is no sign of a pulse, begin chest compressions and artificial respiration (see opposite).

5 Take the baby with you to the telephone. Call 911 or the local EMS.

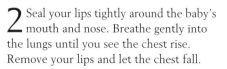

Breathe into the baby's mouth and nose

Breathe until you see the chest rise

2 Seal your lips tightly around the baby's mouth and nose. Breathe gently into the lungs until you see the chest rise. Remove your lips and let the chest fall.

6 Continue giving artificial respiration until help arrives. Check the baby's pulse every few minutes. If the pulse stops, begin chest compressions and artificial respiration (see opposite). When help arrives, call his parents.

BABY NOT BREATHING AND PULSE ABSENT

If the baby is not breathing and the pulse is absent, you will need to breathe into his lungs (artificial respiration) and give chest compressions in order to drive blood around the baby's body.

Place your fingertips on the lower breastbone

1 Place the baby on his back on a firm surface. Place the tips of two fingers on the lower breastbone, just below the imaginary line joining the nipples.

Breathe once into the baby's mouth and nose

Press down on the breastbone to a depth of 1/2-1in (1.3-2.5cm)

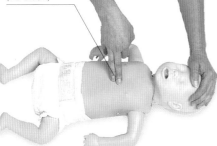

2 When your fingers are in place, press down sharply to a depth of 1/2-1in (1.3-2.5cm). Release the pressure without removing your fingers from the chest. Do this at a rate of at least 100 times per minute (or five times in three seconds). These are chest compressions and they help to drive blood to the brain.

3 Tilt the baby's head back and give one breath of artificial respiration (see opposite, step 2).

4 Give five more chest compressions (see step 2). Follow these with one breath of artificial respiration (opposite, step 2). Repeat this cycle for one minute.

5 Take the baby with you to the telephone. Call 911 or the local EMS.

6 Keep giving five chest compressions followed by one breath of artificial respiration until help arrives, then call the baby's parents.

UNCONSCIOUS CHILD

If a child is not responding to you and you cannot wake her, she may be unconscious (if the child is under one year old, see unconscious baby, page 70). You will need to assess her condition immediately by following the procedure that is set out below.

ASSESS THE CHILD'S CONDITION

1 See if you can rouse the child by calling her name, and gently tapping her on the shoulders. Do not shake the child if you suspect that she might have a spinal cord injury.

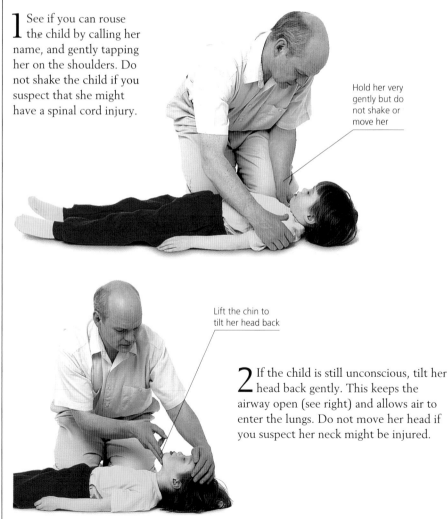

Hold her very gently but do not shake or move her

Lift the chin to tilt her head back

2 If the child is still unconscious, tilt her head back gently. This keeps the airway open (see right) and allows air to enter the lungs. Do not move her head if you suspect her neck might be injured.

Look, listen, and
feel for breathing

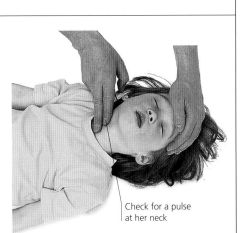

Check for a pulse
at her neck

3 Put your ear near her mouth to listen for breaths and to feel for breath on your ~~c~~eck for 3–5 seconds. Look at her chest to ~~s~~e if it is moving. If she is not breathing, ~~gi~~ve two slow breaths of artificial respiration ~~(se~~e page 77, steps 1 to 3). If the air does not ~~m~~ake her chest rise, give first aid for choking ~~(se~~e page 69) before going on to step 4.

4 Feel for her pulse. Keep her head tilted and feel for the large muscle at the side of the neck. Slide two fingers into the groove in front of this muscle. Press lightly and feel for 5–10 seconds before deciding whether she has a pulse or not.

5 If the child is still unconscious, act according to your findings – see below. If the child regains consciousness, make her comfortable, call 911 or the local EMS and her parents, and watch her carefully.

> **IF** *in doubt, always dial 911 or your local EMS for help.*

Keeping the Airway Clear

Tilting the head slightly brings the tongue away from the back of the throat and opens the passage to the lungs (airway).

Blocked Airway

Tongue
fallen back

Blocked
airway

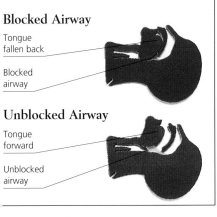

Unblocked Airway

Tongue
forward

Unblocked
airway

• **If the child is still unconscious, but is breathing and has a pulse, treat any life-threatening injuries first, such as bleeding (page 62), or burns (page 60), and then see page 76.**

• **If the child is not breathing, but still has a pulse, see page 77.**

• **If the child is not breathing and the pulse is absent, see page 78.**

CHILD BREATHING AND HAS PULSE

If the child is unconscious, but is breathing and has a pulse, put her in the recovery position, to prevent her from choking.

Bend the farthest leg

Lift the chin to clear the airway

3 Hold the leg farthest from you gently under her thigh with your free hand and carefully pull her knee up to bend the leg, leaving her foot flat on the ground.

1 Kneel beside the child. Tilt her head back – unless you think she may have a spinal injury. This lifts the tongue away from the back of the throat and keeps the air passages that lead to her lungs open.

Gently pull her over onto her side

4 Keep the child's hand against her cheek to support her head. At the same time, pull on the thigh of the bent leg, rolling her toward you and onto her side.

Move the farthest arm across the chest and bend it

Bend this arm and put the back of her hand on the ground

Tilt her head back slightly

2 Straighten her legs. Bend the arm nearest to you so that it makes a right angle. Place the palm of the hand facing upward. Bring the other arm across her chest and hold the back of the hand against her opposite cheek.

5 Adjust her hand under her cheek. Tilt her head back again to open her airway. Bend the top leg into a right angle to prevent her from rolling forward. Call 911 or the local EMS and her parents.

CHILD NOT BREATHING BUT HAS PULSE

If the child is unconscious and is not breathing, but she has a good pulse, you will need to breathe air into her lungs (artificial respiration).

Watch the chest fall

Tilt her head back

1 Lay the child on her back on a firm, flat surface. Remove any object visible in her mouth. Lift the point of her chin with two fingers. If you do not suspect a spinal injury, tilt her head back to open the airway.

3 Remove your lips and watch her chest to see it fall.

4 Continue to breathe into the child's mouth for one minute, giving one complete breath every three seconds (the same as counting twenty breaths per minute).

Feel for a pulse at her neck

5 Stop and check the neck pulse (see page 75, step 4). If it is now absent, begin chest compressions and artificial respiration (see overleaf).

6 Call 911 or your local EMS and continue artificial respiration, at the rate of one complete breath every three seconds, until help arrives.

7 Check the neck pulse every few minutes. If it is absent, begin artificial respiration and chest compressions (see page 78). When help arrives, call her parents.

Blow into her mouth until you see the chest rise

2 Pinch the child's nostrils closed and gently open her mouth. Seal your lips around her open mouth and breathe into the lungs until you see the child's chest rise.

CHILD NOT BREATHING AND PULSE ABSENT

If the child is not breathing and she has no pulse, you will need to breathe into her lungs (artificial respiration) and give chest compressions to drive blood around the body.

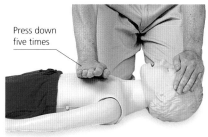

Press down
five times

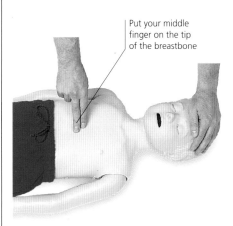

Put your middle
finger on the tip
of the breastbone

1 Lay the child on her back on a firm, flat surface. Find the point where the ribs meet in the middle. Put your middle finger on the tip of the breastbone and your index finger on the bone above it.

3 Using the heel of that hand only, press down sharply to a depth of 1-1½in (2.5-3.8cm). Do chest compressions at a rate of 100 a minute (five in three seconds).

Give one breath of
artificial respiration

4 Give one slow breath of artificial respiration (see page 77). Breathe with enough force to make the chest rise, remove your mouth, and watch the chest fall.

5 Repeat steps 3 and 4, continuing the cycle of five chest compressions to one breath. Repeat this cycle for one minute.

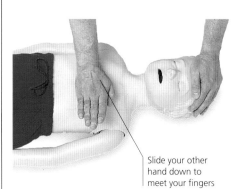

Slide your other
hand down to
meet your fingers

2 Slide the heel of your hand down the breastbone to meet your fingers.

6 Call 911 or your local EMS. Keep giving five chest compressions, followed by one breath of artificial respiration, until help arrives, then call her parents. If she starts breathing, see page 76.

INDEX

ACKNOWLEDGMENTS

Dorling Kindersley would like to thank:
Annelise Evans and Janice Lacock for editorial assistance; Karen Ward for design assistance and help on photography shoots; Jackie Dollar for design assistance; Hilary Bird for the index; Andy Komorowski for set construction; Helen Diplock, Steve Gorton, Miriam Kons and Janice Lacock for loaning props; Habitat for loaning the sofa; and the following for modeling:

Children: Matthew Bartlet, Charlotte Bull, Kashi Gorton, Phoebe Harris, Hannah and Jordan Kons, Hayley Miles, Megan Norwood, Amy Beth Walton.

Adults: Helen Benfield, Helga Evans, Anna Hamilton, Miriam Kons, Philip Ormerod, Jo Walton.

The author would like to thank:
Julie for all her babysitting; Glenda, Lisa and Annelise for all their hard work.

Special effects make-up: Pebbles

Additional photography: Tim Ridley

St. John Ambulance National Headquarters would like to thank:
the Councils of Alberta, Nova Scotia, Prince Edward Island, and Manitoba for their enthusiastic assistance.

For information on how to register for babysitting courses, or how to obtain the best size of first aid kit, contact a local branch of St. John Ambulance.

RECORD AND LOGBOOK

THIS SECTION of the book is designed for parents to fill in and update. Always go through this with your babysitters and discuss any potential problems and answer any questions they have. The book should be left in an accessible place so that the babysitter can refer to it whenever necessary, but make sure it is out of reach of small children. When filling in a page, use a pen that is childproof and has a water-soluble, nontoxic ink. Allow the ink to dry before closing the page. To update a page, wipe it clean with a damp cloth and dry with a tissue.

HOUSEHOLD OBJECTS

WHERE TO FIND	
Diaper equipment	
Baby or children's food	
Cutlery & dishes	
Paper towels, disinfectant	
Snacks, tea & coffee	
HOW TO OPERATE	
Stove/microwave	
Baby monitor	
Television & VCR	
Toaster oven, coffee maker, other appliances	

AROUND THE HOUSE

GAS

The main gas line is...
If there is a gas leak...

WATER

The water shutoff is...
If there is a flood...

ELECTRICITY

The fusebox is...
If there is a power outage...

Where to find a flashlight

HEATING

How to operate it

KEYS

Keys are kept...

TELEPHONE

Telephones are
situated...

If there is no telephone
or if it is out of order...

OTHER

ENTERTAINING THE CHILDREN

Name of child		

FAVORITE ACTIVITIES

Games		
Toys		
Songs/music		
Stories		

TELEVISION

The children are allowed to watch/ time...		
Favorite programs		
Favorite videos		

OTHER

FEEDING AND MEALTIMES

Name of child		

BABIES

Where to find bottles		
How much formula or milk		
Likes formula warm/cold		
What time for feeding		
How to burp baby during and after feeding		

YOUNG CHILDREN USE

Training cup		
Cup		
Spoon; spoon and fork; knife and fork		

FOOD AND DRINK

Snacks & drinks		
Bedtime drink		
Allergies		

OTHER

COMFORTING THE CHILDREN

Name of child		

IF A CHILD IS UNHAPPY

Comforting objects (pacifiers, blanket, toy)		
If a child is upset...		
If a child is hurt...		

SETTLING ARGUMENTS

If children are fighting/arguing...		
If a child argues with you...		
If a child misbehaves...		

OTHER

BEDTIME ROUTINES

Name of child		

GETTING READY FOR BED

Drink or snack before bed		
Time to start getting ready		

Help with changing
        cleaning teeth
        potty or toilet		

Change/put on diaper		

IN BED

Favorite stories		
Favorite songs		
Favorite stuffed toys		
Drink beside bed		
The bedroom door is left...		
The light is left...		

TROUBLESHOOTING

If a child is difficult, try...		
If a child wakes in the evening, try...		
Spare sheets are kept...		
Spare pajamas are kept...		

OTHER

MEDICAL NOTES

Name of child		

ALLERGIES

Food		
Medicine		
Adhesive bandages		
Dust		
Pollen		

INOCULATIONS AND DATES

RECENT ILLNESSES AND DATES

MEDICAL CONDITIONS

Asthma		
Epilepsy		
Diabetes		

OTHER

EMERGENCIES

CONTACT NUMBERS

	Name/Telephone number/Address
Parents	
Doctor	
Relative/friend	
Relative/friend	
Neighbor	
Local hospital	
Local police station	
Taxi	

HOME DETAILS

Telephone number & address

Directions to home for emergency services

BEST ROUTE OUT OF THE HOME IN AN EMERGENCY

WHERE TO FIND

First aid kit/thermometer

Fire extinguishers/fire blankets

IF THERE IS AN EMERGENCY, DIAL 911 OR 0